TYPE
IS BEAUTIFUL

TYPE
IS BEAUTIFUL

THE STORY OF FIFTY
REMARKABLE FONTS

SIMON LOXLEY

Bodleian Library
UNIVERSITY OF OXFORD

First published in 2016 by the Bodleian Library
Broad Street, Oxford OX1 3BG

www.bodleianshop.co.uk

ISBN 978 1 85124 431 7

Text © Simon Loxley, 2016

Images, unless specified on p. 259
© Bodleian Library, University of Oxford, 2016

Cover design by Dot Little at the Bodleian Library
Designed and typeset in 11 on 15 Garamond
by illuminati, Grosmont

Printed and bound in Great Britain by TJ International Ltd,
Padstow, Cornwall, on 90 gsm Munken Premium Cream

British Library Catalogue in Publishing Data
A CIP record of this publication is available from the British Library

CONTENTS

ACKNOWLEDGEMENTS

Thank you to Samuel Fanous for originally proposing the book, and for the help of his colleagues at the Bodleian: Janet Phillips, my editor, and Leanda Shrimpton, picture research and rights. James Mosley, the former long-serving librarian at St Bride Library, very kindly read and gave me his extremely helpful comments on some of the entries. Bob Richardson, Library and Archives Manager, helped with pictures and finding other sources in St Bride Library. For help and information with some of the other entries, grateful thanks to: Caroline Archer, Helen Elletson, Dave Farey, Will Hill and David Shields. Freda Sack (the NatWest fonts) and Juliet Shen (Lushootseed) read and advised me on the entries for their designs and supplied pictures. I'm grateful also to Dennis Bryans, who first made me aware of the fascinating story of *The Chinese Advertiser*, and for his help with information related to it. Andreu Balius (Super Veloz), Vincent Connare, Denis Kovac and Jenny Theolin (Comic Sans), Phil Garnham at Fontsmith (Channel 4 Headline), Alejandro Paul (Piel Script) and Pierre di Sciullo (Amanar) kindly gave permissions and supplied pictures related to their respective entries.

'You have two goblets before you. One is of solid gold, wrought in the most exquisite patterns. The other is of crystal-clear glass, thin as a bubble, and as transparent. Pour and drink; and according to your choice of goblet, I shall know whether or not you are a connoisseur of wine. For if you have no feelings about wine one way or the other, you will want the sensation of drinking the stuff out of a vessel that may have cost thousands of pounds; but if you are a member of that vanishing tribe, the amateurs of fine vintages, you will choose the crystal, because everything about it is calculated to *reveal* rather than to hide the beautiful thing which it was meant to *contain*.

Bear with me in this long-winded and fragrant metaphor; for you will find that almost all the virtues of the perfect wineglass have a parallel in typography.'

Beatrice Warde, *The Crystal Goblet:*
Sixteen Essays on Typography, 1955

A SCRIPT TYPEFACE
expresses the style of a handwritten letterform

serif

A SERIF TYPEFACE
features the 'tab' at the end of strokes

A SANS SERIF TYPEFACE
has no serifs, hence 'sans', French for 'without'

BLACKLETTER
heavy 'gothic' styles, also based on handwritten forms

ascender
the part of the lowercase letter that projects above the x-height

cap height
the height of the **uppercase**, capital letters

x-height
the height of the lowercase x, which defines an upper horizontal visual alignment for the lowercase letters

lowercase
the non-capital letters

baseline
the horizontal alignment upon which the letters 'sit'

descender
the part of the lowercase letter that projects below the x-height

apex

finial
a stroke ending

bowl
the curved stroke that forms the counter

crossbar

a bracketed serif meets the stroke in a curve

an unbracketed serif meets the stroke at an angle. This example also shows a square-ended slab serif

counter
the 'hole'

tail
a curved descender

spur

stroke or stem

arm

ligature
two or more joined characters. Here the finial of the f also represents the dot – or **tittle** – of the i and avoids the collision of those parts if the letters were separate

ear

leg

link

chiselled

loop

inline

INTRODUCTION

Why are there so many typefaces? Justification for their
number has been given in the past by making comparison
with songs or varieties of wine, more of which the world is
always happy to accept. But it has also been pointed out that if
a designer or visual communicator had no desire to influence
people in some way, then we would only need one typeface.
The 2007 feature-length film about a single typeface, Gary
Hustwit's *Helvetica*, contained interviews with designers who
insisted they indeed only ever used one typeface, Helvetica,
seen as an efficient, essentially baggage-free font that released
them from what they saw as a valueless and time-consuming
part of the design and conceptual process, choosing a typeface.
But Helvetica, like all the others, was designed with a purpose
and a philosophy, and carries these in its DNA, while collecting additional cultural associations as it makes its way through
our lives. As an illustration of this in the same film, for the
designer Paula Sher, Helvetica was inescapably entangled in her
mind with the corporate America that supported the Vietnam
War and by implication all of the United States' unresolvable
conflicts since.

Type itself was originally simply the means by which printing could take a quantum leap in the ease of dissemination of
ideas and information – in the first instance, the Bible – and,
if all went according to plan (which it didn't), make its European instigator Johann Gutenberg a comfortable fortune on
the way. Except that it wasn't that simple even then. Gutenberg
created his type in imitation of a north German handwritten
form with which he and his readers were already familiar, a
familiarity that would speed acceptance and a swifter financial

return on his otherwise radical offering, a multiple-copy product for a world accustomed to unique, handwritten books (GUTENBERG'S BIBLE TYPE). Yet fifteen years later in southern Europe what we would now term type designers looked to different models to style their type. That of Nicolas Jenson and others in Venice was cultural, political even (JENSON'S ROMAN TYPE; ALDINE ITALICS). The words themselves might be as inviolate as the accuracy of the proofreading would allow, but already the type was starting to tell the reader an additional story by association.

It's a capability to which the human subconscious seems remarkably welcoming. Children from an early age recognize graphic symbols and logos, and accurately associate them with the items they represent. A similar recognition of a typeface, a lettering style, doesn't come far behind. We don't as readily realize this because we're busy reading the words. But it's there.

Typefaces communicate moods and feelings: some are considered elegant or refined, while others seem bold, radical or whimsical. Typefaces can reflect the fashions or the zeitgeist of an era, often to a surprising degree. Some typefaces were created for a specific purpose. Some are easy to read and draw little attention to themselves; others are meant to grab your attention, but only for the purpose of a few words. Which font is chosen for any given communication matters a great deal, since it conveys a whole world of meaning, both blatant and subliminal, and much time, thought and money continue to be spent to try to get it right. These messages are part of the story of each typeface in this book.

Type in Europe began in the mid-1400s. Before this, books were handwritten by monks or professional scribes, and what ephemeral printing there was would have been created by xylography, printing from a reverse image cut from a single block of wood. 'Type', what became known as 'moveable type', meant individual characters which could be assembled into a chosen order, and held together in that configuration so that they could be placed onto the bed of a printing press, inked, multiple prints made from them, then disassembled for a different future text.

Unsurprisingly there were numerous subsequent claims as to which country was the birthplace of printing, and who was the inventor. Agreement has now settled on Johann Gutenberg in Mainz, Germany, although he also lived and worked in Strasbourg, France. By the 1470s the focus moves to Venice, which became the catalyst for new typographic letterforms and, vitally, innovations and developments in publishing, with some of the significant typographic energy being supplied by craftsmen moving south from France and Germany. At this point Venice was the capital of the Venetian Republic, then at the height of its powers; its territories encompassed large areas of northern Italy, parts of the Dalmatian coast, and numerous holdings in the Aegean. There was wealth from trade, not least with the Far East, and relative liberalism, there being no censorship in the republic until the middle of the sixteenth century, with freedom of worship and accompanying political asylum. In this environment the publishing industry thrived: here we see the emergence of seriffed roman type and italics that are still, in their essential forms, dominant today, a cultural shift away from the heavy blackletter used by Gutenberg in imitation of the formal scripts of northern Europe (FRAKTUR).

Although the exact method by which Gutenberg made his type is still a subject of debate, type at this period and for the next five hundred years was made of metal, a mixture of which the largest part was lead. The starting point for the creation of a piece of metal type was the punchcutter, who would sculpt the image, in reverse, of the letter or character into a hard metal, usually steel. This was the puncheon, usually known more simply as the punch, and was the most crucial stage of the process. How good the resulting typeface was, depended on the skill of the punchcutter. Numerous factors might affect the final inked image of the character on the paper; quality might well be lost. But no quality could be gained en route if the punch was poor to begin with.

The punch would be hammered into a softer metal, usually brass or copper, to create the 'strike', the matrix, containing an indented positive image of the character. The matrix would be fitted to a type mould, which, when filled with molten metal, provided the 'body' of the piece of type. When the metal hardened, the piece of type was produced, once again a reverse image of the character, in relief on its body of metal. This uppermost surface constituted by the character, when inked and applied to the paper, resulted in a final, positive image.

England's first printer, William Caxton, set up his printing press in Westminster in 1476, but in terms of quality of printing and typography, Britain would stand in continental Europe's shadow until the 1730s (CASLON).

The eighteenth-century Age of Enlightenment can be seen as a period in which the intellect was brought to bear on printed letterforms, a reassessment of their visual impact on the page of a book, and the contribution that their styling might make to this. Although the type's visual appearance was of equal importance to Gutenberg, his approach was, of necessity, imitative. In the eighteenth century Pierre-Simon Fournier in France, John Baskerville in Britain and Giambattista Bodoni in Italy all showed a desire to change or develop what had gone before, controlling and manipulating the effect of their own type designs on the printed page (BASKERVILLE; BODONI).

Britain's political stability in the eighteenth century, following the turbulence of the years under the Stuarts, brought increasing prosperity. The onset of the Industrial Revolution and the avoidance of invasion during the Napoleonic Wars placed the country in a strong commercial position in the early nineteenth century. Type now found a new terrain and role, not just as text on a page, but used large, in competitive headlines for posters and street advertising. The many vigorous styles emerging during this period sought, sometimes frantically, for novelty, to stand out. They have suffered periods of scholarly revulsion, but are now very much back in favour (FAT FACE ITALIC; POUCHÉE'S 18 LINES NO. 2).

Until the late nineteenth century, the method of setting type, picking individual characters out of a type case and assembling them by hand, had remained essentially unchanged in four hundred years. But an increase in levels of literacy led to a greater demand for printed output, and innovation was needed. It came in the form of two systems developed in the United States: Linotype, which made its debut at the *New York Tribune* in 1886, and Monotype, patented the following year. A keyboard transmitted information to casting machines, which contained the matrices and created the type within the machine. After use, the type – individual characters with Monotype, in conglomerate form (literally a 'line o' type') with its rival – could be melted down ready for the next task. This caused a crisis among traditional typefounders, who saw demand for their wares, cast type, diminishing rapidly. In the United States a number grouped together for support, amalgamating into American Type Founders. The company, looking for ways to increase sales, vigorously developed the concept of the type family, with multiple weights which could be used by advertisers to emphasize different elements of their copy.

Increased demand had led to a perceived fall in quality, the result of a combination of stylistically inappropriate letterforms with the abandonment of printing craft standards in pursuit of profit. This led William Morris in Britain to found his own private press, the Kelmscott Press, and to design his own types (GOLDEN TYPE). He inspired what would be called a private press movement, in which the leading players deemed a custom-designed typeface a necessity (DOVES TYPE). Type companies also began to look to pre-nineteenth-century designs which had fallen from favour, reviving them to perform within the new technology. The often crude, unsophisticated energy of nineteenth-century sans serif advertising types, 'grotesques', was given classical roman proportions and a new dignity by Edward Johnston for London Underground (LONDON UNDERGROUND). The sans serif was further developed in Germany and later Switzerland, to accompany and project sometimes a whole new philosophy that encompassed not just printing and design but, later, society as a whole (FUTURA; HELVETICA).

By the late 1950s, typesetting was experiencing another revolution, with the gradual emergence over the subsequent two decades of photosetting as the dominant commercial method, the matrices being replaced by photographic negatives which produced the type as a photographic image. This proved to be a short-lived, interim technology, with the arrival of the desktop computer in the 1980s. The uncertain future of the Apple Macintosh was saved by a 'killer app', a page layout program, sparking what became known for a while as DTP, desktop publishing. This of course needed typefaces.

So began type's fourth technological age, and a golden one, in which typefaces became more commonly known as fonts. As well as greater ease of use for designers, removing the middleman of the designated typesetter, the digital age has seen an explosion of creativity and new type designs. It has simply become much cheaper and easier to design and market a new font. The early twenty-first century has also seen exciting new designs, not just from Europe and the United States, but from Latin America, particularly beautiful and exuberant reconfigurations of what had long been a vibrant Hispanic style, the script (PIEL; ZULIA).

And what of the type designer? Today the vast majority of designers will have followed the conventional route of some sort of higher education on a visual arts course, but until the latter half of the last century this would have been the exception. Frederic Goudy worked as an accountant and in real estate; Stanley Morison was a bank clerk; Louis John Pouchée was a restaurant owner and coal merchant; William Thorowgood went into the type business after a lottery win; the first William Caslon's apprenticeship was as a loriner, a maker of metal parts for horses' bridles; Frederic Warde abandoned medical training. For some, from Gutenberg onwards, it was, so far as we can tell, a career path chosen for financial motives. For others it was, or became, almost a spiritual calling. The separate status of type designer, as distinct from printer and probably also publisher, was a later development, just as the status of 'graphic designer' was synonymous in most people's minds with 'printer' until the 1920s, notwithstanding the efforts on his own behalf of Bruce Rogers (CENTAUR).

For several of the faces in the selection here, the person we would designate the designer is unknown. The vast majority of those that are known are men. The world of printing and design was, like so many others, a male-dominated one. Beatrice Warde, Monotype's publicity manager for several decades, had to conceal herself behind a masculine pseudonym to have her writing on the subject of typography taken seriously (GARAMOND). But it was a world in which women played a part, sometimes to a surprising extent, given the age in which they lived. Following the death of William Caslon II in 1778, the foundry was run by his widow Elizabeth. After a schism with one son, the third William, she continued in tandem with the widow of another. Sarah Baskerville produced a specimen of her husband's types following his death. Bodoni's wife Paola Margherita Dall'Aglio finished his magnum opus, the *Manuale Tipografico*, similarly after her husband's death. In the first half of the twentieth century, the British Monotype company's products sometimes only worked properly as typefaces following careful interpretation and development of less-than-perfect designer drawings by its largely female drawing office.

And there are now, of course, female designers who have built significant reputations, such as Carol Twombly and Zuzana Licko. Arguably one of the advantages of type's democratization in the digital era is that it has been taken out of the formal, structured and traditionally male-dominated workplace. Anyone with the ability and the software can now produce a font design and market it, on their own working terms.

The Internet seems to have made the world even fonder of lists and chart placings than ever. Nick Hornby's 1995 novel *High Fidelity* affectionately mocks its central characters, the staff of a record shop, for their obsession with creating Top Fives, what was then assumed to be a solely masculine tendency to try to put the world into some sort of order by evaluating and grading aspects of it. Typography has not been immune to this. The arrival of the personal computer took awareness of fonts, their different names and different qualities, out of the preserve of graphics industry specialists and placed it within the reach, and the hands, of everyone. With that came popular use, and, in the eyes of some, popular misuse, which in turn has led to sometimes vociferous online judgements as to what constitutes good and bad, and an increased general awareness of the cultural references associated with each font.

This book isn't intended to be a 'fifty best'. There are no chart placings. I chose the typefaces selected for the book on the basis that they ticked at least one of the following boxes:

¶ They are part of the typographic 'canon'; they are accepted classics, enduring mainstays 'tried and tested' as options for text or headline use.

¶ They are significant in the history of type and design for what they represented or caused to happen, rather than intrinsically for what they themselves were.

¶ They have helped, or were created with an intention to help, people in some way.

¶ They add style to something that, in the opinion of the author, is culturally important, or they have assumed a cultural significance in themselves.

¶ They came to encapsulate, by becoming a kind of visual shorthand, a stylistic era or time period, or a certain idea or philosophy.

¶ They are – again, in the opinion of the author – beautiful.

A bonus to the above would be that the typefaces possessed a fascinating story attached to their history or development. Of these, I can confidently say, the book is not in short supply. I hope you will enjoy reading it.

For each inclusion I have given a 'first appearance' date. Although for many it is hard to pinpoint this with certainty, I have tried to give a date, where possible, of when the design was first given some sort of public showing, whether this was just as a sample setting or a specimen, rather than when it was actually designed, a process which might run over a period of years.

Historically, the term 'designer' for the type's aesthetic creator is not entirely appropriate for the earlier designs, as it is a term that, in delineating a specific role in the process from concept to printed impression, only emerged in the early twentieth century. But for the sake of uniformity, I have retained it for every entry.

GUTENBERG'S BIBLE TYPE

FIRST APPEARANCE   ABOUT 1454, GERMANY
DESIGNER   WORKSHOP OF JOHANN GUTENBERG,
POSSIBLY CUT BY PETER SCHÖFFER, GERMAN

We'll start right at the beginning – in terms of type, that is. The concept of what was called moveable type – the means of assembling representations of individual letters that could be configured into words and sentences, have a printed impression taken from them, then be disassembled and reconfigured to make new words – had a precedent of some limited use in China and Korea around the end of the first millennium and the start of the second, but didn't appear in Europe until the middle of the fifteenth century. For reasons of national prestige, there have been several candidates put forward and sometimes vigorously championed as the inventor of moveable type in Europe: Johann Mentelin in Strasbourg; Jean Brito in Bruges; Pamphilo Castaldi in Feltre, Italy; and, the most forcefully trumpeted of all contenders, Laurens Coster in Haarlem in the Netherlands. Then there is the mysterious Procope Waldfoghel, an itinerant goldsmith who appeared in Avignon in the 1440s offering instruction in a form of mechanical writing using metal letters, then disappeared from history after leaving the city to escape his creditors.

What connects some of these stories is that they contain links, or legends, of what would now be termed industrial espionage – or downright theft – of the knowledge of the craft of printing, its techniques and even materials, that lead back to Mainz, and to someone called Johann. Johann Gensfleisch zur

Laden zum Gutenberg is now almost universally credited with being the inventor of European printing, but the evidence is largely circumstantial. No piece of printing bore his name. No likeness of him exists which was made in his lifetime. Later portraits show him, as Gutenberg scholar Victor Scholderer has written, 'in a furred cap such as might have been worn by a Polish nobleman, with a forked beard … as a patrician … [he] would have been clean shaven'. The date of his death is known, 1468, but estimates for his date of birth range from the early to mid-1390s, to the early years of the fifteenth century. But although Gutenberg himself is a shadowy figure, he is first cited as the inventor of printing as early as 1472. Although this of course is insufficient in itself, Gutenberg appears in surviving legal records on several occasions and for various reasons – one of them a breach-of-promise suit. The information contained in these has allowed scholars to build a convincing case for him. He seems the most likely candidate, by some distance.

Some accounts associate Gutenberg's father with the episcopal mint in Mainz; if this is correct, then working with precious metals formed part of the family's background. Political infighting in 1428 resulted in the exile of some of Mainz's patrician class. Gutenberg was listed in a 1430 amnesty allowing him to return, but there is no evidence he did at that point. In 1434 he was involved in the arrest of a Strasbourg official for non-payment of money owed. The breach-of-promise suit came in 1436, with an additional fine for Gutenberg's slandering of one of the witnesses.

The story starts to acquire focus in 1439. Gutenberg had set up a small working partnership, one of whose members had died of the plague, with the result that his brothers wanted to take over his share of the business and, blocked in this

ncipit ꝓlogus beati ieronimi
ꝓsbiteri; in libros machabeorum·
achabeoꝝ libri duo pno=
rant prelia·inter hebreoꝝ
duces gentemꝗ persarū:
pugnā ꝗ sabbatoꝝ·τ no=
es machabei ducis triūphos:eꝝ cui⁹
ie τ libri idem sūt nūcupati·Hec ꝗ
toria cōtinet etiā inclita illa gesta
achabeoꝝ fratrū: qui sub antiocho
e pro sacris legibus dira tormenta
ꝓessi sunt. Quos mater pia dum
versis supplicijs urgeret non solū
fleuit:sed et gaudes hortabat ad
ria passionis. Explicit ꝓlogus
cipit liber primus machabeorum·

T factū est postꝗ per=
cussit alexander phi=
lippi reꝝ macedo qui
primus regnauit i
grecia egressus de ter=
ra cethim dariū regē
farū τ medoꝝ·constituit prelia multa:
obtinuit omniū municiones·et in=
fecit reges terre. Et pertransijt usꝗ ad
es terre:τ accepit spolia multitudinis
ntū:τ siluit terra in cōspectu eius. Et
gregauit virtutē τ exercitū fortem ni=
is : et exaltatū est et eleuatū cor ei⁹:et
ninuit regiones gentiū τ tyrannos
facti sunt illi in tributū. Et post hec
idit in lectū:τ cognouit quia more=
ur.Et vocauit pueros suos nobiles
i secū erant nutriti a iuuentute sua:
diuisit illis regnū suū cum adhuc
ueret. Et regnauit alexander annis
rodecim:τ mortu⁹ ē. Et obtinuerūt
eri ei⁹ regnū unusquisꝗ i loco suo:
imposuerūt omnes sibi diademata
st morte ei⁹ τ filij eoꝝ post eos annis
tis: et multiplicata sūt mala i terra.
t exijt eꝝ eis radix peccati·antiochus

illustris fili⁹ antiochi regis qui fuerat
rome obses:et regnauit in anno cen=
tesimotricesimo et septimo regni greco=
rum.In diebus illis exierunt eꝝ isrl filij
iniqui:τ suaserūt multis dicentes. Ea=
mus τ disponamus testamentū cū gen=
tibus que circa nos sūt : quia eꝝquo
recessim⁹ ab eis inuenerūt nos multa
mala. Et bonus visus ē sermo i oculis
eoꝝ. Et destinauerūt aliqui de ꝓo τ
abierūt ad regē : et dedit illis potestatē
ut facerēt iusticiā gentiū. Et edificaue=
rūt gymnasiū in therosolimis secūm
leges nationū·τ fecerūt sibi preputia:τ re=
cesserūt a testamēto sancto·τ iuncti sūt
nationibus: et venūdati sunt ut facerēt
malū. Et paratū ē regnū in conspectu
antiochi:τ cepit regnare i terra egypti:
ut regnaret super duo regna. Et intrauit
in egyptū in multitudine graui in curri=
bus τ elephantis τ equitibus:τ copiosa
nauiū multitudine. Et constituit bellū
aduersus ptolomeū regē egypti:τ veri=
tus ē ptolomeus a facie eius τ fugit:
et reciderūt vulnerati multi. Et compre=
hendit ciuitates munitas in terra egy=
pti:τ accepit spolia terre egypti. Et con=
uertit antiochus postꝗ percussit egyptū
in centesimo τ ꝗdragesimo τ tercio an=
no τ ascendit ad isrl:et ascendit ihero=
solimis i multitudine graui. Et intrauit
in sanctificatione cū superbia:τ accepit
altare aureū τ candelabrū luminis τ
uniuersa vasa eius τ mensam proposi=
onis τ libatoria τ fialas τ mortario=
la aurea τ velū τ coronas τ ornamen=
tum aureum qd in facie templi erat:τ
cōminuit oīa. Et accepit argentum τ
aurū et vasa cōcupiscibilia:et accepit
thesauros occultos quos inuenit: et
sublatis omnibus abijt i terrā suā. Et
fecit cedem hominū: et locutus est in

initiative, had taken the matter to court. The partnership had been involved in two enterprises, polishing gemstones and making devotional mirrors (believed capable of catching and storing benevolent powers from the reflection of holy relics) for sale to pilgrims on their way to Aachen for a forthcoming pilgrimage. Unfortunately they had got the date of the event wrong by a year, so with time on their hands they urged Gutenberg to instruct them in what was referred to as 'the adventure and the art'. Gutenberg, even before his colleague's death, had been extremely protective of this third venture, giving instructions to melt down 'forms', a term later used for types. There was also a mysterious object which a servant had been instructed to disassemble into four pieces so that no one would know what it was. Gutenberg scholars have speculated – though whether with wishful thinking – that this was possibly a mould, for casting metal type.

In 1448 Gutenberg reappeared in Mainz, and borrowed on an increasing scale: first a loan of 150 Rhenish guilders; then in 1449 or 1450 he entered into an agreement with a figure who becomes notorious in the Gutenberg legend, the lawyer Johann Fust, who lent him 800 guilders. Scholderer tells us that this amount would have bought '100 fat oxen or several sizeable farms in the Mainz of the 1450s'. This was for 'finishing the work'. In November 1455 an action was brought by Fust against Gutenberg for defaulting on payments for this and a subsequent loan of similar amount. Perfecting a radical new way of disseminating knowledge, the effort of which ran over several years, was unsurprisingly proving an expensive under-taking. Fust had become Gutenberg's business partner as well as financier for 'the work of the books'. The court ruled than Gutenberg should repay the original loan plus interest. When he was unable to do so, the business and all the equipment passed into Fust's hands, who then went into partnership with the gifted punchcutter Peter Schöffer, in all probability already a member of Gutenberg's workshop. Little more is known of Gutenberg after this date. In 1458 he defaulted on some old Strasbourg debts; in 1465 he was granted a pension by the prince-archbishop of Mainz. His 1468 will bequeathed printing equipment to what was probably another financial supporter.

Although there are earlier items which are believed to be examples of Gutenberg's printed output, 1455 was a significant year for more than just Fust's legal action, because it probably marks the appearance of what became known, because of the number of lines of text on the page, as the 42-line Bible, 'B42'. Aeneas Silvius Piccolomini, the future Pope Pius II, wrote in early 1455 that he had seen in Frankfurt in October 1454 sections of a Bible printed clearly enough to read without glasses, and that the number produced was 158, or 180.

Gutenberg's Bible is regarded by many as still the most beautiful book ever printed. Gutenberg's motives for producing it would, unsurprisingly in view of the financial commitments he had to make, have been almost entirely commercial. But he was hoping to exploit a growing market. With an increase in literacy in the fifteenth century, and with new institutions of study and learning being founded across Europe, there would be a need for books that could not be met by the existing method – handwritten by monks or scribes – which was slow and very expensive.

But a book like the Bible, and in the page size in which B42 was produced, would have been aimed at a higher, more affluent market than students. If Gutenberg was to succeed in making that market accept a new product produced by a means that meant that the item was not, as other books in their possession, unique, then it would be easiest if its appearance followed as closely as possible the style of what was currently in existence. This is the solidly practical reason why Gutenberg's type looks as it does, imitating as closely as it can the written hand of German scribes.

Exactly how his type was made, its very nature, has been a matter of intense scrutiny and debate, and is likely to remain so. Was it cast in sand? Was it actually modular, combinations of strokes rather than whole characters? Some estimates put the total number of letters and typographic elements, known as sorts, in his typecase at around 270. This number would include ligatures and abbreviations – sometimes signs that represented a combination of letters, but usually a letter with an accompanying mark to signify missing letters. These, too, followed practices already established by scribes. The liturgical books of the region were written in what is classified stylistically as the blackletter subgroup 'textura', characterized by narrow, tightly set letterforms which carry a strong emphasis on the verticality of their strokes. Their beauty comes from this even, rhythmic visual stress. To achieve this, word spacing needs to be kept tight and regular. Gutenberg's Bible has short line lengths in relation to the size of the type, set in two columns per page, and these abbreviations were necessary to achieve this required evenness.

The appearance of the B42 type is further enhanced by the ink with which it is printed, described as resembling more an oil paint than a printers' ink as we would know it, containing copper, sulphur and lead, and resulting in a dense blackness with a sheen to it. Some headings in the early parts of the Bible were also printed in a second colour, red, again following manuscript style, but the feature was quickly abandoned, undoubtedly through cost and time considerations. Coloured elements – rubrication – including page decorations, and also the binding of the Bible, fell upon the purchaser to commission and specify.

Forty-eight copies of the Bible, in varying states of completeness, were known to have survived into the twentieth century (there is one in the Bodleian Library); since then, the Second World War resulted in two copies located in Leipzig never being seen again, presumably destroyed, and a further two broken up and sold as separate 'leaves', a practice now discredited. Gutenberg's type, beyond its intrinsic beauty and the skill and craftsmanship that went into the production of the Bible, stands as the conduit, the medium through which the spread of knowledge and information, for both good and evil, would flow across Europe and beyond.

JENSON'S ROMAN TYPE

FIRST APPEARANCE   1470S, ITALY
DESIGNER   NICOLAS JENSON, FRENCH

Jenson's type is built on the proportions that would prove a benchmark for subsequent roman designs. It was to Jenson that William Morris turned, seeking to reconnect type design to its classical foundations, away from what he saw as the aberrations of the nineteenth century (*see* GOLDEN TYPE). And it was to Jenson that Emery Walker and Thomas Cobden-Sanderson of the Doves Press returned for their type, in an attempt to strike closer to Jenson's ideal than Morris had (*see* DOVES TYPE). Bruce Rogers used Jenson as his model for Montaigne and, in an attempt to better this first effort, for Centaur (*see* CENTAUR). How did this French printer end up in Venice at the end of the fifteenth century, and why has his roman type had such an enduring influence on print culture?

The spread of printing in Europe, if one adopts Gutenberg in Mainz, or even Strasbourg, as a starting point, took in the following years a significant southward journey to Italy. Its early practitioners, however, were foreign migrants. Conrad Sweynheym and Arnold Pannartz are credited with being the first printers in Italy, producing an edition of Cicero's *De Oratore* at Subiaco near Rome in 1465. The Benedictine monastery where they set up their press contained some Germans, which may have been the reason for them being allowed to print there. Sweynheym was from or from near Mainz, inevitably and perhaps accurately rumoured to have worked for Johann Fust and Peter Schöffer (*see* GUTENBERG'S

ITERMINAI O GIOCOND
imperadore con epistola forfe di tr
narrarti elibri della historia natural
uella alle mufe romane:nata apref
lultima genitura.Sia adunq; quef
uerissima di te metre che gia inuec
dissimo tuo padre : per che usand
Catullo mio compatriota tu soleu
re qualche chofa le mie ciacie. Tu c
sta castrense & militare parola.Et l
sai mutando le prime syllabe si fe
piu duro che non uolea essere stim
familiari & serui . Per questo adur

nai scriuerti:& achora per che le nostre chose apparischino & sieno manife
mia audacia maxime doledoti tu che pel passato non lhabbi facto in una
procace epistola.Et accio che tutti glhuomini sappino quanto di pari lom
uiua: Tu elquale hai triomphato & se stato censore & sei uolte cosolo &
la tribunitia potesta:Se stato prefecto del pretorio:ilche hai facto piu nol
glaltri magistrati:perche per piacere a tuo padre & allordine equestre lac
tutte queste cose per rispecto della republica hai facto : Et me chome nel c
castrense tractasti? Et certo niete ha mutato inte lamplitudine & grandez
fortuna:se non che tanto piu possi & uogla giouare:quato quella e magg
beche a tutti glaltri huomini sia aperta la uia a impetrare ogni chosa da te
Niente di meno solo laudacia fa che io piu familiarmente te honori. Qu
adunq; imputerai a te medesimo:& a te medesimo nel nostro fallo perdo
stroppicciai la faccia:& niente di meno nessuno proficto ho facto: perche
uia mapparisti grande:& di lontano mi rimuoui con le faccelline del tuo i
certo in nexuno piu ffolgora quella:laquale piu ueramente e decta in te c
za deloquentia.In te e quella facundia che alla tribunitia potesta si conuie
risonantia tuoni tu le laude paterne? Co quanta(non sanza amore)dimo
tuo fratello:Quanto se excellente & sublime nella poetica faculta ? O gra
danimo. Certo hai trouato inche modo possi imitare tuo fratello . Ma
chi potrebbe sanza paura considerare : hauendo a uenire al giudicio
tuo : maxime essendo quello dame prouocato ? Certamente non sor
conditione quegli che publicano alchuno libro:& quegli che ate glintitol
che se io lo publicassi & non lo intitolassi ate:potrei dire perche leggi tu q
imperadore:lequali sono scripte albasso uulgo & alla turba de glagricult
tefici & a quegli che cosumano elloro otio negli studii?Perche adunq; ti f
concio sia che quando io scriueuo questa opera:non thaueuo posto nella
sono descripti egiudici:Et eri di tanta excellentia : che non stimauo che t
scendere si basso:Preterea quando bene non fussi in si excelso grado:nien

BIBLE TYPE). But the centre of late-fifteenth-century printing and publishing would not be Rome, but Venice.

Venice in the late fifteenth and early sixteenth centuries was, with Paris and Naples, one of three European cities with a population of more than 150,000. It was also the capital of the Venetian Republic, whose territories at its height encompassed about a third of northern Italy, with considerable holdings on the Dalmatian coast and in the Aegean, including Crete and Cyprus. Within its borders both Verona and Brescia had over 50,000 citizens. Venice itself has been evaluated as more important in world terms than Italy is today, and may have been the richest city in the world. Venice was wealthy through trade, not just with Europe but with the Middle and Far East. By the standards of the era it was relatively liberal and tolerant, and took in foreigners and those seeking asylum, with communities of Greeks, Armenians and Jews. As a result there was a vibrant, energetic business culture. It is this capacity for business, allied with finance and a literate population, that together helped Venice become a publishing powerhouse. By one calculation, publishers working there had by the end of the fifteenth century produced some 4,500 titles.

Johannes da Spira (also known as von Speyer or, with his first name italianized, as Giovanni) was also from Mainz; he and his brother Wendelin (Vendelino) were the first printers in Venice, producing another work by Cicero, *Epistolae ad Familiares* in 1469. The types used by both Sweynheym and Pannartz and the da Spiras displayed a definite stylistic shift away from the blackletter of Gutenberg. Sweynheym and Pannartz's was something of a halfway house, melding characteristics of both styles, the da Spiras' a more definite roman. So distinctive were they that Giovanni da Spira secured an exclusive right to use roman letters for five years – 'a vast improvement' on the Subiaco type, 'but not an absolute invention as was boldly claimed by the brothers', writes Stanley Morison in the introduction to his *Four Centuries of Fine Printing*. In the light of what was to come next, it is unsurprising that the type's actual creation has been credited to the man who would became Venice's most celebrated Renaissance printer, Nicolas Jenson.

Jenson (*c.* 1420–1480) was also not Italian. Born in the Champagne region, he worked in the mint in Paris, and became master of the mint at Tours, experience of working in metal before he came to type. It seems likely that Jenson was sent by the French king Charles VII to Mainz in the late 1450s to find out about the printing being undertaken there, and bring back what he had learned with a view to beginning printing in France. There is no evidence that he did this, and he appears instead in Venice a decade later. As well as a putative collaboration with the da Spiras, he is also linked, in some accounts, to Sweynheym and Pannartz. But his opportunity to build a reputation for himself came in 1470. This was the year Giovanni da Spira died, with little time to enjoy his monopoly on his roman type; the restriction ended with his death, and in the same year Jenson produced an edition of Eusebius' *De Evangelica Praeparatione* using for the first time type that could definitely be ascribed to him (*see* CENTAUR).

Jenson's output over the next ten years is regarded as having made Venetian printing pre-eminent. Morison describes the type in Jenson's first book as 'more mellow' than the da Spira model. Although the actual presswork of Jenson's books fell short of excellence, it is the type, the typesetting and the layout that earn him his reputation.

Where Jenson's sense of proportion failed him was in the relation of his upper case to the minuscules. Morison pinpoints these as being too large, creating a 'spottiness' on the page, and he is right. It's a shortcoming that Morris and the Doves both replicated, but Rogers avoided. The imbalance – if such it is, for it is ultimately a question of personal aesthetics, or even chronological perspective – is perhaps unsurprising. Given the examples of upper case that Jenson could draw upon – the domineering, extravagant capitals of blackletter, illuminated initial letters, the magisterial majuscules of roman inscriptions – all assert the primacy of the upper case.

But, leaving aside this question, Jenson's achievement was to lay down a set of ground rules, of illustrations in terms of the drawing of letterforms, their proportions, their weight, their relation to each other, that would serve as a standard of excellence both for his own time, and for the centuries ahead.

THE ALDINE ITALICS

FIRST APPEARANCE 1500, ITALY
DESIGNERS ALDUS MANUTIUS, FRANCESCO GRIFFO, ITALIAN

Without the italic, typography would be visually the poorer, and in practical terms, in its primary aim of communication, severely compromised. Some commentators ascribe a purely financial motive to the publisher who brought about this innovation in print, a means of reducing overheads on a planned series of books. But of course the creation of significant contributions to the world, whether culturally, aesthetically or for the improvement of the human condition, are often driven by the need or desire to make money, if only to pay off one's debts, as Johann Gutenberg would have recognized (*see* GUTENBERG'S BIBLE TYPE).

Aldus Manutius is not just known for the introduction of the italic, however. He has also been credited with printing the first best-seller, creating the idea of reading for entertainment, and being the first to use the semicolon. It's an impressive list. Like Nicolas Jenson, he both benefited from and in turn enhanced the unique social and literary environment that was the Venetian Republic in the late fifteenth century (*see* JENSON'S ROMAN TYPE).

Aldo Manuzio, or, as he is more commonly known in the Latin form of his name, Aldus Manutius, was born in about 1449 at Bassiano in central Italy. He studied in Rome with the scholars Gaspare da Verona and Domizio Calderini. He later worked as a private tutor, and it was not until he was nearly forty years old that he would move into the field of activity for which he would be remembered. He moved to Venice and worked for the publisher and printer Andrea Torresano, who had previously worked with Jenson. It was schooling in both disciplines, printing and publishing, for Manutius, and in 1495 he produced his first book as a publisher, Constantine Lascaris's Greek grammar, the *Erotemata*. The Latin and Greek classics would become the speciality of the Aldine Press, its considerable output in the field distinguished by the accuracy of its texts and the scholarship brought to them by Manutius's editors.

Manutius provided a fruitful well of material for future type revivalists, by virtue of the new roman type with which he printed the 1496 Latin dialogue *De Aetna* by the Venetian scholar Pietro Bembo, and that used in the *Hypnerotomachia Poliphili* (1499), an illustrated dream allegory by the monk Francesco Colonna. Stanley Morison drew on both sources for his Monotype revivals in the 1920s, Bembo from the former, Poliphilus from the latter. The *Hypnerotomachia* is regarded, both visually and also, increasingly, for its content, as a high point of early printed books; even, alongside the Gutenberg Bible, one of the twin peaks (*see* GUTENBERG'S BIBLE TYPE).

The fifteenth century saw a growth in literacy in Europe and in institutions of learning, expanding the market for printed books which made viable the technological development of printing in the middle years of the century. Manutius wanted to produce the classics in smaller-sized editions affordable for new types of reader – students, and former students, now lawyers, doctors and teachers, who either needed or wanted their own books, small enough to be easily portable, to be carried to study or for periods of repose and recreation. It was a new publishing concept – the pocket edition. To make it financially viable, Manutius increased his print runs. To make

INFERNO.

El mezzo del camin di nostra uita;
n   Mi ritrouai per una selua oscura;
Che la diritta uia era smarrita:

E t quanto a dir qual era, è cosa dura   *esta .*
Esta selua seluaggia et aspra et forte;
Che nel pensier rinuoua la paura.

T ant'è amara; che poco è piu morte.
Ma per trattar del ben, ch'i ui trouai;
Diro de l'altre cose, ch'i u'ho scorte.

I non so ben ridir, com'i u'entrai;
Tant'era pien di sonno in su quel punto,
Che la uerace uia abbandonai.   *ucrace.*

M a po ch'i fui al pie d'un colle giunto   *pie.*
La, oue terminaua quella ualle,
Che m'hauea di paura il cor compunto;

G uarda in alto; et uidi le sue spalle
Vestite gia d'e raggi del pianeta,
Che mena dritt'altrui per ogni calle.

A llhor fu la paura un poco queta;   *queta.*
Che nel lago del cor m'era durata   *lago del cor.*
La notte, ch'i passai con tanta pieta.   *pieta. i. lam*

E t come quei; che con lena affannata   *simil do*   *tento*
Vscito fuor del pelago alla riua   *lena i an*
Si uolge a l'acqua perigliosa, et guata;   *elito .*
                                                 guata.
C osi l'animo mio, ch'anchor fuggia,
Si uols'a retro a rimirar lo passo;   *retro.*
Che non lascio giammai persona uiua.

P o c'hei posat'un poco'l corpo lasso;   *hei i. habui.*
Ripresi uia per la piaggia diserta,   *deserta*
Si ch'l pie fermo sempr'era'l piu basso.   *pie.*

SCHOLAR'S COPY: AN ANNOTATED EXAMPLE OF THE ALDINE PRESS
EDITION OF DANTE'S *DIVINE COMEDY, LE TERZE RIME DI DANTE,* 1502.

it physically viable, the most popular theory goes, he needed to fit more words on the page; and by means of what was in intention a condensed typeface, Manutius had a new design cut by the punchcutter Francesco Griffo that was slightly inclined and based on a cursive script. The italic was born.

But type historian Harry Carter, in *A View of Early Typography* (1969), has pointed out that, 'If Aldus hoped, as it is commonly said that he did, but he never said, that cursive letterforms would save space, he must have been disappointed by the result: a roman type on the same body gets in just as much.' Looking at an example of the type, this view seems hard to disagree with. Carter felt that the reason for Manutius's new type was more likely to be stylistic, a less formal letterform for a less formal edition. But again the underlying motive could have been financial, the aim of making these smaller, cheaper books look distinctive, special – small but beautifully formed. Carter points out that stylistically the form had been in existence for at least three-quarters of a century, comparing it to the written hand of scholar Niccolò Niccoli.

Although Manutius's italic is considered to be significant for being the first rather than the best, the sales of the new small editions, an addition to the series being produced every two months for five years, were so robust that the type became widely seen, and inevitably copied. Manutius tried to protect the concept by taking out what was effectively a copyright, granted to him by the Venetian Senate. But pirate versions were soon appearing, particularly in France. Manutius therefore also became a pioneer in suffering from font piracy, the curse of the type designer ever since.

Whether this plagiarism was a tribute to the type, or merely attempts, by visual imitation, of unscrupulous parties to assume at least the aura of the rigorous scholarship for which the Aldine editions were famed, is impossible to say. But by this process the style embedded itself in the typographic landscape, and perhaps came to be seen as a more suitable medium for expressing the poetic spirit.

Manutius married Torresano's daughter, some decades his junior, and continued publishing until his death in 1515, the health of his business waxing and waning largely in tandem with the political fortunes of the Venetian republic, which became decidedly chequered during these final years of his life. But his reputation has not just survived, but has been enhanced through the subsequent centuries as a result of both his editorial and his visual contributions, a giant cultural legacy.

Where would the type family, that muscular business concept of the early twentieth century, be without the italic? Yet in some ways the type family is a compromise, based on an arguable willingness to ignore the evidence of one's eyes. With many sans serifs the italic is really little more than a sloped version of the regular form, and in terms of contrast can suffer as a result. But it is a clear development of the design. Serif italics generally have far more visual contrast, to the extent that it could be argued that they are in fact a different typeface altogether. They are designed to fit with the roman in terms of weight and certain features, but we merely accept the convention that they are essentially the same typeface. Visually they don't really resemble each other at all. Whether William Caslon (*see* CASLON) would have regarded the 'italicks' shown in his type specimens as bearing any connection to the romans he offered, beyond matching each in size, is debatable.

An example of this disparity remains with us. What is now known as Centaur Italic actually started life as an entirely separate face, Stanley Morison and Frederic Warde's Arrighi, which had been a revival of one of the cursive types of Manutius's Italian contemporary, the former papal scribe Ludovico degli Arrighi (*see* ARRIGHI). Centaur's designer Bruce Rogers, when approached by Monotype to make a commercially available version of his design, professed himself unable to design an accompanying italic and suggested Arrighi, a face he'd admired and, as a book designer, had already used. Both Centaur and Arrighi were redrawn in 1928 to work together when released the following year by Lanston Monotype.

FRAKTUR

FIRST APPEARANCE   EARLY SIXTEENTH CENTURY, GERMANY

Strictly speaking, although there has been at least one typeface
called simply Fraktur, the word is actually a generic term for
a certain style of blackletter, the heavy angular faces, typified
in Britain by Old English, that are based on the broad-nibbed
pen style of medieval monks and scribes (*see* CLOISTER BLACK).
Other styles of blackletter, such as bastarda or rotunda, are
more calligraphic, or more open in the shapes of the letters.
As Judith Schalansky says in *Fraktur Mon Amour* (2006), her
beautiful and compendious blackletter overview and visual
index: 'Fraktur integrates round with broken forms … austere,
and adroit, courtly and bourgeois … they tend to dominate
the blackletter faces, hence the common use of Fraktur as a
collective name for the entire typeface group.' As the name
means 'broken script', one might add to her description adjec-
tives such as 'heavy', 'angular', 'jagged', and, in reference to
the descenders, 'dagger-like'. Fraktur remains the style we most
immediately think of in terms of blackletter, in its extreme
manifestations beautiful but also frightening – but that reaction comes from associations in its past.

And blackletter, in particular as a type style, carries those
associations with it. As Schalansky says in her introduction,
'While blameworthy usages roll off the abstract forms of
Futura like water off a duck's back, messages seem to cling
much more easily to blackletter's differentiated lettterforms.'

Type historian Harry Carter, in *A View of Early Typography*
(1969), places Fraktur as the last of the medieval writing styles

ONLY ONE OF SEVERAL CULTURAL CONNECTIONS OF THE STYLE, BUT
PROBABLY THE ONE THAT LOOMS LARGEST: THE THIRD REICH.

to take typographic form, pinpointing its first appearance in the accompanying texts to Albrecht Dürer's engravings in the 1522 *Triumphwagen Kaiser Maximilians*, and credits the design of what would become the type to the calligrapher Johann Neudörfer.

Carter was an admirer, calling Fraktur 'a courtly taste of the highest secular majesty ... a frozen cursive' – frozen by virtue of its upright structure, unlike the more relaxed, cursive blackletter style such as bastarda, and austere in comparison with textura, the upright style under which Gutenberg's Bible type is defined (*see* GUTENBERG'S BIBLE TYPE).

Blackletter, although the style used for Europe's earliest printed books, quickly became a northern European style, in contrast to the roman letters created with such finesse by Nicolas Jenson (*see* JENSON'S ROMAN TYPE) and which became associated with the Renaissance and progressive thought. William Caxton, England's first printer, used blackletter, but his assistant Wynkyn de Worde, who took over the business after Caxton's death, later printed using roman type, and by the seventeenth century blackletter was largely restricted to use for emphasis, performing the role of a modern bold weight. If in its regional popularity blackletter was associated with the Protestant north of Europe, and roman more with the Catholic south, in parts of central and south America the association today is actually the reverse, the type having been brought to the New World by the Spanish, their use bringing with it connections of faith, piety and good fortune through heavenly benison.

By the nineteenth century Germany was the only region in Europe still using blackletter for text. There it took the role of symbol of national identity. In the early decades of the century Germany was still a patchwork of independent kingdoms and duchies, which during the Napoleonic era endured for periods subjugation to French rule. Notwithstanding, the debate over the perpetuation or abandonment of its usage continued in Germany into the early twentieth century. Although in the 1920s it was Germany where the exciting developments in design and design philosophy were taking place, and where progressive sans serif designs were appearing, blackletter still held its position. That became stronger in the 1930s. Adolf Hitler, gathering support for the Nazi Party in his attempt to gain power through the legitimate route of the ballot box, was aware of the need to court the more rural, conservative sections of the electorate, and declared blackletter to be the true German letterform. Although Futura's designer Paul Renner believed it to be more of a French style (and indeed its continuing popularity on shop fascias in northern France and Belgium suggests he may have been right), he was to suffer repercussions as a designer of a sans serif type.

Ironically it was the Nazis themselves who were to end blackletter's use in Germany, declaring in 1941 that the style had Jewish origins, and was now forbidden. The underlying reason for this may have been more practical: roman made it easier for the populations of western Europe to read edicts from the occupying power. Equally, Hitler's judgements became increasingly erratic and illogical as the war continued, so he may well have actually believed the official statement.

It is the Nazi connection that has given Fraktur its power in the seventy years since the end of the Second World War. Of the blackletter styles, it is the one that is the heaviest, the most aggressive in appearance. A pariah in its own land following the war, it is this typographic outsider status that has caused it to be adopted by groups as diverse as heavy metal bands, rappers and R&B artists, and skateboarders. Like Cloister

Black, it's a popular lettering style for tattoo artists, not least for its illustrative qualities. With tattoos now commonplace, Fraktur has effectively moved back into the mainstream. Judith Schalansky's book can itself be seen as an attempt to reassess and reposition the style. Fraktur can be judged as ugly. Of the blackletter styles, it is the one in which one imagines the Third Reich's most brutal orders to have been set. But remove this connection, which was after all imposed upon it, and it can be seen also to possess beauty, albeit one that does not necessarily court legibility. But whatever its merits or lack of them, a style that can take on so many sometimes conflicting associations, and continue to be popular in the face of all practical argument, has to have a claim to greatness.

GARAMOND

CLAUDE GARAMONT'S TYPES   1540S, FRANCE
DESIGNER   CLAUDE GARAMONT, FRENCH

JEAN JANNON'S TYPES   ABOUT 1621, FRANCE
DESIGNER   JEAN JANNON, FRENCH

Since its arrival as a commercially available typeface in the late teens and early twenties of the twentieth century, Garamond has been an enduring favourite as a text choice, and has crossed the technologies, from metal, through photosetting to digital, adapting to each, and arguably growing in strength in the process. It's a matter of taste, of course, but Francesco Simoncini's 1961 reworking, or Robert Slimbach's 1989 Adobe Garamond version, softened the nervous energy of Monotype's 1922 italic, making it easier on the eye, with more open counters (the spaces inside the letterforms) and a pleasingly rhythmic inclination to the bowls – the curved sections of characters like the a, b and q. Garamond roman is both elegant and delicate, yet robust, distinctive with its top-seriffed finials on the T, and the angled link on the g. Even the International Typeface Corporation (ITC), which customized – to questionable benefit – most of the classic faces with their policy of imposing large x-heights and stubby ascenders and descenders, were unable, in their 1977 version, entirely to mar Garamond's grace.

But the story behind Garamond is a more complex one, involving two cases of concealed identity, and type history's most famous detective story. Whether that particular story

A REMARK OF SOCRATES

I regard that man as devoid of understanding who rests capable of taunting another with his poverty *or of valuing himself on having been born in affluence.*

PAGES FROM AN ELEGANT GARAMOND SPECIMEN PRODUCED BY LANSTON MONOTYPE, 1923.

N.B.

As a contribution towards the revival of old styles which characterizes the printing of our day The Lanston Monotype Corporation, Ltd., in addition to reproducing the Garamond type for the first time in Great Britain, has cut a series of special italic ligatured characters, swash letters & special "final" sorts which will be valuable in instances where it is desired to create a very definite antique character. A number of these forms have for generations been unobtainable from any source, whether English, Continental or American.
A display will be found on the following page

should be filed under fiction, non-fiction or scripted reality, we may never fully determine.

Claude Garamond (d. 1561) or Garamont, his own spelling of his name, was a French punchcutter and publisher, to whom was attributed the type known as the Caractères de l'Université, which were owned by the Imprimerie Nationale, the national printing office of France. The rush to revive the face started in the early twentieth century. In 1917 Morris Fuller Benton produced the American Type Founders' Garamond, based on the Université letters. In 1922 the British Monotype version appeared. Frederic Goudy designed Garamont for Lanston Monotype in America, which appeared in 1923. The German foundry Stempel's arrived in 1925. These had all been preceded by a version cut by the Parisian foundry Ollière in 1913.

In January 1925 Beatrice Warde (1900–1969), formerly the assistant librarian at the American Type Founders' celebrated company library in New Jersey, and her husband Frederic, arrived in England, Frederic initially to work on some projects with Monotype's typographic advisor Stanley Morison, a collaboration that, before it soured dramatically, resulted in the Arrighi typeface (*see* ARRIGHI; TIMES NEW ROMAN).

Subsequently the long-serving publicity manager for Monotype in Britain, Beatrice was adroit at personal mythology. According to her own account, ATF librarian Henry Lewis Bullen had given her the job in preference to applicants offering actual qualifications because she had a letter of recommendation from the designer Bruce Rogers (*see* CENTAUR). He handed her a duster and told her to get to work on the books. She was also allowed to open any that caught her eye. As the library was never inundated with visitors she had ample study time, and began building up a personal store of typographic knowledge. Writing ran in the family; her mother May Lamberton Becker was a writer on children's literature and a columnist for the *New York Herald Tribune*.

Morison had taken over the editorship of the typographic journal *The Fleuron* entirely from his fellow founding editor Oliver Simon, and needed assistance. It was he who had persuaded the Wardes to make their Atlantic crossing, and one plan was to use them as contributors to the journal. Frederic contributed 'On the Work of Bruce Rogers', with whom he had worked in New York, an article which, although her husband largely assembled and structured the material, was probably written for the most part by Beatrice. If this was the case, then 'Frederic Warde' was her first nom de plume. The second was Paul Beaujon. The prospect of a woman writing on typography and being taken seriously was seen as unlikely in the male-dominated professional landscape of the 1920s. She later wrote:

> So far all my work had been done under the pseudonym of Paul Beaujon, partly because there was one Warde already, and partly because nobody at that time had any idea that a woman could possibly know anything about printing, typography or such like. So the name Paul Beaujon was invented with great care to conceal the personality of the actual writer … curiosity was really aroused when he produced an article about the Garamond types.

Beatrice began work on that article in 1925. Again according to the legend, there was a nagging recollection from her time at the library:

> Bullen had once shown me a specimen of the American Type Founders' version of Garamond and had said, 'You know, this is definitely not a sixteenth-century type. It is based upon the type at the Imprimerie Nationale, which is itself *attributed* to Garamond, but I have never found a sixteenth-century book

which contained this typeface. Anyone who discovers where this thing came from will make a great reputation.

As she told it, Beatrice's article had been already typeset for *The Fleuron* when she came across an item in the Bagford Collection of title pages in the British Museum. Her suspicions aroused, she raced to Paris, did further swift research, then amended the article. It appeared in *The Fleuron* no. 5 in 1926 as Paul Beaujon's 'The "Garamond" Types: Sixteenth and Seventeenth Century Sources Considered'.

In the article, after an overview of Garamont's career and types, she concluded that the type at the Imprimerie, upon which nearly all the twentieth-century revivals had been based, had in reality been the work of Jean Jannon (1580–1658), a Paris-based printer who moved in 1610 to Sedan where, as a Protestant, he worked for a Calvinist academy. He was a punchcutter as well as a printer, and had cut the smallest type yet known. Jannon had produced a type specimen for the Sedan Academy in 1621. By 1644 he was working for a wealthy merchant based in Caen, Pierre Cardonnel, who had aspirations as a publisher.

Printing in France in the seventeenth century was as strictly controlled as it was in England (*see* CASLON), and two documents Beatrice cited in the archives of the Bibliothèque Nationale told her subsequent story. The press was raided by the king's officers, and the punches and matrices confiscated. Beatrice believed that they then became the property of the newly founded Imprimerie Royale. (In fact some of Jannon's matrices had been bought by the Imprimerie Royale in 1641.) They were attributed to Garamont in the mid-nineteenth century, and revived for use, with additional sizes cut, at its end. She also believed the Jannon provenance might explain the rather mysterious name, as the type had no connection with Paris's Sorbonne university. She argued that the academy at Sedan was a university, although legally prevented from calling itself such, and that Jannon may well have named the type himself.

Although Beatrice's article was the result of serious research on her part, it seems likely that in reality she had some assistance in which directions to direct her lines of enquiry, the pattern of which was probably somewhat different to those outlined in her neat and fortuitous recollection. On the first page of the article she acknowledges the Garamont scholarship of Jean Paillard, who 'succeeded in ranging all the documents then known and some new material in a small privately printed book of admirable scholarship'. Cited in her footnote, the book in question is *Claude Garamont, Graveur et Fondeur de Lettres: Étude Historique* (*Claude Garamont, Engraver and Letterfounder: Historic Study*). It had been published by the Parisian foundry Ollière in 1914, using types cut the previous year under Paillard's direction, based on type that was actually Garamont's. There was a sound reason for this, because in the book Paillard himself had thrown doubts on the provenance of the Caractères.

Stanley Morison had acquired a copy of this book in late 1924. The Wardes sailed to Europe at the New Year, but instead of arriving in England, their new home, they went to Paris to meet Morison. Before the month was out Beatrice's husband Frederic was writing excitedly to Bruce Rogers telling of 'interesting and enlightening information about Claude Garamond', which would be 'revealed in *The Fleuron*'. In another letter to the Boston printer Daniel Berkeley Updike he sketched Paillard's title page, so keen was he to show what he had. He bought what sets he could find of the pages of Paillard's book, unbound as was still a widespread French publishing practice, and had them bound and sent to his correspondents. It seems very likely that Beatrice was aware of another writer's previously expressed doubts as to the attribution of the Caractères from when she first set foot in Europe.

The *Fleuron* article did, as Bullen had purportedly predicted, make a reputation. In 1973, after Beatrice's death, the type historian Harry Carter, in his additional note to the Garamond entry in the revised edition of Stanley Morison's 1953 *A Tally of Types*, wrote:

> The article by Beaujon owed a good deal to one by Jean Paillard, *Claude Garamond, Étude historique*, published in 1914 by the Parisian typefounder Ollière. Paillard was the first to challenge the attribution of the Caractères de l'Université to Garamond. His essay has not been given the recognition that it deserved.

Paillard had died in action near Verdun in September 1914, and the Ollière foundry was also gone by the time Beatrice wrote her article. But although Beatrice could arguably have been franker about the nature of her sources, we shouldn't perhaps be too hard on her. She was trying to gain entry into a world unsympathetic and resistant to female contribution. On a personal level, by the middle of 1926 her marriage looked increasingly unstable (she and Frederic separated in November), leaving her in even greater need of her own income. The article did its work, and gave Beatrice Warde the academic weight she needed to secure her post at Monotype. The twentieth-century typographical world would have been a drabber one without her (*see also* the excerpt from *The Crystal Goblet* which opens this book).

CASLON

FIRST APPEARANCE   1720S, GREAT BRITAIN
DESIGNER   WILLIAM CASLON I, BRITISH

Any pantheon of classic typefaces would have to include Caslon. Making its first appearance in the 1720s, it dominated that century. Although it then gradually dropped from popularity, it was revived by a couple of discerning printers in the middle of the nineteenth century, enough to put it back on the radar for those looking for types to revive in the early twentieth century, and it has been a stalwart, particularly as a text face, ever since.

Redrawn to fit prevailing trends and aesthetics, and changing technology, reconfigured, returned to its roots: Caslon just feeds off the attention, and its position as a type classic is now assured. It carries a feeling of solidity, a lack of pretension, that many commentators have admired. In the 1920s American printer and type historian Daniel Berkeley Updike compared it favourably with its British contemporary Baskerville for just this quality. In 2013 designer Jeremy Tankard, looking to pinpoint the quality of 'Britishness' in type design to channel into a new design of his own, found Caslon's characters to conform to a geometry of circles and squares, a no-nonsense beauty built on very logical principles. The capitals in the earlier metal versions are a little too weighty in relation to the lower case, but this only adds to the type's rugged sophistication. Its accompanying italic has a distinctive presence all its own, a jagged insistence – tight, condensed, with a pronounced inclination.

A SPECIMEN

y W. CASLON, Letter-Founder, in Chiſwel-Street, LONDON. 1742.

CASLON'S TYPE SPECIMEN OF 1742. HIS ORIGINAL ROMAN DESIGN HAD BY THIS POINT BEEN DEVELOPED INTO A RANGE OF SIZES.

Caslon's original creator was William Caslon (1693–1766), the founder member of what became a typefounding dynasty, and usually referred to as William Caslon I to distinguish him from his similarly named descendants. Born in Halesowen, he became an apprentice with the Worshipful Company of Loriners in London in 1706; a loriner, or lorimer, made the metal parts for horse bridles, but this was not the area of activity for which Caslon was destined. The Caslon company eventually created its official legend to describe how it came into being; although the sequence of events and motivations of some of the players have been called into question by subsequent research, as legends tend to be, there is a neatness to the story and probably an essential truthfulness. Instead of busying himself with equine accoutrements, Caslon worked as an engraver of gun locks, an area of the metal body of a firearm which could be embellished by ornamental work on the surface of the metal. He was also a sculptor and engraver in metal of ornamental stamps for bookbinders. His work caught the eye of the printer John Watts – who would later give employment to the young Benjamin Franklin on his first sojourn in England – and the printer and publisher William Bowyer, who, together with a third sponsor, set Caslon up in business around 1720 as a typefounder, believing that the skills he demonstrated might be transferred to the cutting of typographic punches. In view of the current poor standard of English type, it was hoped that a quality product would find a hungry market.

The timing was right. England had recently emerged from a century of turmoil; the fallout from the religious schism of the Tudor period, civil war, the deposing and execution of a monarch, the establishment and fall of what was in essence a republic, what was in everything but name a Dutch invasion, and another monarch driven from the country. A printed item, rather than representing perhaps a piece of recreational reading, signified potential trouble for the presiding power, and it needed control. All books had to be licensed, and entered in the Stationer's Register, and had to carry the name of the author, the printer and the publisher. Contraventions could be brutally punished by imprisonment, crushing fines and bodily mutilation. The right to produce type and to print was heavily restricted, and those granted the privilege were not necessarily the best qualified. In 1694 restrictive legislation lapsed, and it was possible to publish without permission, which meant considerably less fear of retribution. There was a consequent growth in newspapers in the early years of the eighteenth century. But in the preceding decades there had been little incentive for excellence in type design or manufacture. The Monotype company's typographic advisor Stanley Morison's *Four Centuries of Fine Printing*, originally published in 1924, showed no examples from Britain that pre-date the eighteenth century. The good type was imported; the bastion of quality in printing was mainland Europe, France and the Netherlands in particular. John Fell, the vice chancellor of Oxford University, in his efforts to improve the output of the University's press in the 1670s, first imported Dutch type, then brought in a punchcutter from the Netherlands to produce what later became known as the Fell types.

Enter William Caslon, and back to the legend. He was approached in 1722 by the Society for Promoting Christian Knowledge, which wanted to print a New Testament and Psalter for the benefit of poor Christians living in the Middle East (*see* CASLON'S ENGLISH ARABICK). Caslon was commissioned to cut an Arabic fount. The Society was pleased with the result; but significantly, at the foot of the specimen he produced he printed his own name in a roman letter. Impressed, the printer Samuel Palmer suggested to Caslon that he cut the whole fount. So positive was the reaction to Caslon's Pica Roman that the flow of type into Britain was reversed; by the 1730s Caslon was exporting type, and within decades numerous competitors to Caslon, sometimes disaffected ex-employees, had set up in business. Caslon's success even spread to the Empire and beyond; the American Declaration of Independence and the United States constitution were both set in Caslon.

Caslon wasn't an innovator in terms of type design; his success was based on quality. A comparison of the letterforms of Caslon's 1734 specimen with, for example, the type in Joseph Moxon's *Mechanick Exercises* of 1683, which gave instruction on typefounding, immediately reveals the enormous leap forward that Caslon achieved. He drew heavily, in both his roman and its accompanying italic, on existing Dutch forms to create his letters. Similar features can be seen in the Fell types. The great innovation of the Caslon dynasty came with William Caslon IV's Two Lines English Egyptian of 1816, the first known example of a commercially available sans serif type (*see* TWO LINES ENGLISH EGYPTIAN). Caslon's Pica Roman is classified as an Old Style type, with less of a contrast between the thick and thin strokes than the later Transitional and Modern styles. Interestingly, a comparison of different sizes of the Caslon roman in eighteenth-century specimens reveals that corresponding letters are by no means exact copies varying only in scale. There can be what a modern type designer would consider very pronounced stylistic divergences. But, to use a modern term, the DNA of the type is always there, like dogs of the same breed but of different colour. It suggests as well, perhaps, that Caslon's eye wasn't stimulated so much by a hard and fast style, as by feel and crispness of execution. But it would be unrealistic to imagine that an eighteenth-century typefounder would think in the same way as a twentieth- or twenty-first-century designer. In the end it doesn't matter; what William Caslon I and subsequent generations produced speaks to us still in a new millennium. As the American type designer Oz Cooper (*see* COOPER BLACK) said, 'If William Caslon had improved his types as much as they have since been improved by others they would not have endured, for sleek perfection palls on the imperfect persons who buy and use type.'

CASLON'S ENGLISH ARABICK

FIRST APPEARANCE   1725, GREAT BRITAIN
DESIGNER/PUNCHCUTTER   WILLIAM CASLON I, BRITISH

William Caslon's 1734 type specimen, along with its subsequent versions, is remarkable not only for the quality of the master punchcutter's letters, but also for the range of linguistic possibilities it offered (*see* CASLON). As well as numerous sizes of his celebrated roman face and its accompanying italic, Caslon's list carried a Greek face in four sizes and a Hebrew in three. Both languages would have been familiar to an academic readership studying the works of classical authors, or for those engaged in biblical and religious studies. But Caslon had also cut one size each of 'Coptick', Armenian, 'Syriack', Samaritan and 'Arabick'. The early eighteenth century might be imagined as an age of slow enough communication within the British domestic market, with little or no interest in the languages of non-European societies. But Britain in the eighteenth century was an outward-looking nation. With Scotland and England unified and stabilized under the constitutional monarchy of the Georges following the turbulence of the previous century, Britain was now able to extend its power globally, to trade and to colonize. Caslon's own success was made possible by this stability, and it was a growing prosperity to which he contributed. There was clearly enough profit in the market for Caslon to have cut these faces; one in particular plays a major part in the Caslon legend and in his success, and the effect that success had on the world around him.

The knowledge and study of Arabic in England during the seventeenth century was not great; it had been a language with a European presence during the dominance of the Moors in the Iberian peninsula, which came to an end with the fall of the kingdom of Granada to Christian Spain in 1492. The Arabic scholar William Bedwell (1561–1632) had a fount of Arabic type cut to print the results of his researches, left on his death to Cambridge University, which never carried out his wishes in this respect. John Greaves's *Bainbrigii Canicularia* (1648) and Edward Pococke's *Specimen Historiae Arabum* (1649) were the first two books published using Arabic type by Oxford University Press. By the early eighteenth century, probably the leading English scholar in the language was Simon Ockley (1678–1720), who published the first volume of his *The Conquest of Syria, Persia, and Egypt by the Saracens* in 1708.

The Society for Promoting Christian Knowledge was founded by an Anglican priest, Thomas Bray, and others, in 1698, and claims to be, after Oxford and Cambridge universities, the third oldest publisher in England. It pursued printing and publishing activities from early in its existence, and determined not to confine its efforts solely to territories where there were English commercial or colonial interests. It became involved with the Danish Mission to Tranquebar – now Tharangambadi – in southern India, arranging the reprinting and shipping of Bibles in Portuguese, and in 1711 had sent a printing press, type, and materials including paper, plus a printer, whom they had trained but who didn't survive the journey. Using the press the missionaries printed a Tamil edition of the New Testament in 1714.

When the Society decided to publish and print an Arabic Psalter and New Testament for distribution in the Middle East, it engaged the Damascus-born scholar and teacher

Salomon Negri from the University of Halle in Germany; as well as teaching, he worked on Arabic publications for the SPCK. According to some accounts, the idea for the project came from his suggestions.

Again, according to the Caslon legend, the commission to cut the Arabic face for the Society's Bible was his first, although if this was the case why did the Society choose him above more established figures? The records of the Society's committee meeting in June 1722 state that Caslon was recommended by the bookseller and philanthropist Thomas Guy, who gave generously to St Thomas' Hospital in London and was the founder of Guy's Hospital. A fellow benefactor to St Thomas' was the merchant Thomas Hollis, who around this period founded the first two professorships at Harvard University. One of Caslon's benefactors, William Bowyer, was a printer for Hollis, so it is possible that this was the line of connection. The Society's founder Thomas Bray also had connections with the Caslon family's home town of Halesowen.

The Psalters and New Testaments were to be printed by Samuel Palmer in London, using a new casting by Thomas James's foundry of the 'polyglot' Arabic fount used for the London Polyglot Bible of 1657. The size of the Polyglot Arabic was Great Primer, about 17 point. Negri was critical of some of the characters, and James had had to have them recut. But it was then calculated that printing the Bible using type at this size would exhaust the Society's available funds. A week after his recommendation, Caslon was invited to attend the next meeting and met Negri, who asked him to cut some sample letters. Two weeks later he brought back his sample, which was approved by Negri. It was estimated that 300 characters would be needed, in a smaller size, English, about 13.5 point, and that this would constitute six months' work for Caslon.

English Arabick.

لا يلي لك الاٰ آخر غيري ❈ لا تاٰخذ لك صورة ❈ ولا تمثيل كل مـــا

فـى السّماٰ من فوق ❈ وما فى الارض من اسفل ❈ ولا ما فـى

المـاٰء من تحت الارض ❈ لا تسجد لهنّ ❈ ولا تعبدهنّ ❈

لانّي انـا الربّ الاٰهك الاٰ غيور ❈ اجتزي ذنوب الاٰباٰء من

At least in the early months of the work, Negri visited Caslon twice a week to advise and to inspect progress. By late January of the following year, however, Caslon had not finished, and asked the Society, in view of the financial outlay which the task had involved, to advance him 20 guineas to prevent him having to take on other work to survive financially. Apart from a few extra requests, most of the work was finished by the end of 1723. In the end Caslon had cut 355 punches, with an extra six characters cut directly into the copper of the matrices. The Psalter appeared in 1725 and the New Testament in 1727.

During this time Caslon had clearly been working on other things too, as he was able to append his name in Pica Roman to the Arabic specimen. It is to this action that Caslon and his subsequent dynasty owe their success and fame, and by which the standard of British type was raised beyond that of its previous continental superiors, and was exported to North America. In this context Caslon's English Arabick has to be regarded as a significant, pivotal face. But on its own terms, was it any good? Type historian James Mosley, in his 1967 article 'The Early Career of William Caslon', has stated that even to someone unfamiliar with Arabic it is clearly inferior to that used in the book given to Caslon as a model by Negri – which he had identified as the Medici Press's 1593 edition of the works of the Persian polymath Avicenna, the type in which had been cut by Robert Granjon. Johnson Ball, in *William Caslon: Master of*

Letters, offers some defence of Caslon's version in that it would have not been a direct copy of Granjon's, but a modification under Negri's instructions and wishes, and salutes Caslon's achievement in producing a set of characters that met the requirements of a foremost scholar of the day but that, to the punchcutter himself, would have been an entirely alien set of forms.

But Caslon's English Arabick, regardless of its own merits, was, if we are to believe the Caslon legend, a chance and indirect catalyst for propelling its maker to typographic stardom. Without Caslon and his descendants' pre-eminence in the remainder of the century and beyond, the history of type would look very different to us today.

BASKERVILLE

FIRST APPEARANCE   1754, GREAT BRITAIN
DESIGNER   JOHN BASKERVILLE, BRITISH

John Baskerville stands alongside the first William Caslon
as one of the two typographic giants of eighteenth-century
Britain (*see* CASLON). Both created typefaces that have become
classics, pillars of the typographic canon of text faces, and
both came from the English Midlands. Thereafter direct
comparison becomes less straightforward. Caslon's type was
more robust in appearance and its effect. Use of Baskerville
introduces, subtly, an essence of something else, something
a little more mannered, perhaps a slightly self-conscious
elegance. But both are time-tested enhancements to the page,
and work effectively at headline size too.

The personal stories of their respective creators differed too.
Caslon went to London. Baskerville remained in Birmingham
all his life. Caslon founded a dynasty, whereas Baskerville's
typefounding didn't long survive his death. Caslon almost
single-handedly created the British type industry, while Baskerville remained an outsider. Caslon, a typefounder, essentially
followed the style of existing letterforms, doing them superla-
tively well. Baskerville was an innovator, in type design, paper,
ink and printing methods, a publisher and printer. Baskerville
didn't just design his type; he created a whole world for it to
live in on the page.

He was born in 1706. His early life is largely obscure; one
subsequent commentator on his life related that Baskerville
had told him he'd 'made his way from a livery servant to

considerable property'. He was later a writing master – a beautiful slate with examples of his lettering styles survives – but he made his fortune in japanning, in the eighteenth century a highly popular lacquering process which could be applied to a wide range of items: furniture, metal household objects, picture frames, buttons. By the late 1740s he was able to buy considerable property and grounds in what is now central Birmingham and turn his attention to a new passion, printing.

Looking at much of the printing around him, Baskerville concluded that it would be pointless to create meticulously crafted letterforms if the ink with which they were printed, and the paper on which they were printed, could not satisfactorily display and enhance those forms. So he set about trying to improve every aspect of the printing process, creating both his own very black ink, which may have owed something in its production to the methods of japanning, and smoother, whiter paper, possibly achieved by a process involving heat and pressing.

Baskerville's type first appeared in book form in his 1757 edition of Virgil's *Bucolica, Georgica et Aeneis*. It is usually classified as Transitional in style, in that he created a greater contrast between the thick and thin strokes than is evident in Old Style types such as Caslon's, but the contrast was not as extreme as the later Modern style (*see* BODONI). There is an elegance, a roundness of form. The italic is gentler, lacking the condensed energy of Caslon's. If more comparisons were to be drawn, Baskerville's type might be described as feminine to Caslon's masculine.

Indeed, comparisons *were* drawn at the time, not least by Baskerville himself, in his preface to his 1758 edition of Milton's *Paradise Lost*: 'In [Caslon's] great variety of Characters I intend not to follow him; the Roman and Italic are all I have

PUBLII VIRGILII

MARONIS

BUCOLICA,

GEORGICA,

ET

AENEIS.

BIRMINGHAMIAE:

Typis JOHANNIS BASKERVILLE.

MDCCLVII.

LETTING IN THE LIGHT: THE TITLE PAGE OF BASKERVILLE'S FIRST BOOK,
VIRGIL'S *BUCOLICA, GEORGICA, ET ÆNEIS*, PUBLISHED IN 1757.

hitherto attempted; if in these he has left room for improvement, it is probably more owing to that variety which divided
his attention, than to any other cause.' Many of his contemporaries were less positive. His friend and supporter Benjamin
Franklin, then living in London, wrote to Baskerville telling
how a visitor had said 'you would be a means of blinding all
the readers in the nation; for the strokes of your letters, being
too thin and narrow, hurt the eye, and he could never read
a line of them without pain.' Franklin later offered the same
critic a Caslon specimen under the guise of it being Baskerville's work, and gained the same response. Baskerville was
not unjustified in believing there was some prejudice towards
him as an industry outsider. He wrote to the president of the
Royal Academy of Sciences in Paris in 1773: 'I have never sold
any types, nor do intend to sell any to London printers, as my
labours have always been treated with more honour abroad
than in my native country.'

Even after two and a half centuries of wide and often
dramatic developments in graphic design and visual communication, the impact of encountering one of Baskerville's
title pages remains undiminished, and it is here that the full
effect of his type is felt. Using nothing but type and space, he
created what was in essence a house style for his publications,
austere yet sensual, simultaneously stark and lavish. The effect
is created in part by Baskerville's supporting players – the
tone and texture of his paper, the colour of his ink, the crispness of impression – but also, of course, by the shapes of the
letterforms themselves. It is an effect which, if responded to
positively, remains little short of breathtaking in its graphic
power. Baskerville himself was fully conscious of this potent
yet delicate ambience created by his letters, which needed,
in his opinion, an unadulterated environment in which to

operate. He wrote to a French printer in 1773: 'As to the last Request of giving you two lines of each size of my characters to insert in your intended work, I reply'd that I had but one objection to it, & that was that it was not in your power to do them justice when us'd with other types...'

In consideration of Baskerville's achievements, writer and printer Francis Meynell in his *English Printed Books* (1946) provides a superb analysis of his methods:

> He achieved amplitude not merely by handsome measurement but by letting in the light ... Look at the title page of his Virgil. It seems no more than a series of lines of capitals centred one over another, as by a combination of logical arrangement and formula. But this is artifice at a height: the art of concealing the care and the sense of balance which has taken infinite pains to obtain the right interlinear spacing and letterspacing, the right gradations of size.

Baskerville, a man who rode through the streets of Birmingham in a golden coach, created a visual wealth and opulence on the printed page by an exact reversal of his performance in the street, by stripping away ornament and, in most cases, any consideration of colour.

His type found greater favour among contemporaries in Europe, particularly France, and was an inspiration to Giambattista Bodoni in Italy. But, although Baskerville became disgruntled at what he perceived as his own lack of domestic recognition in the field, even in Britain late-eighteenth-century faces like that of newspaper owner and publisher John Bell arguably owed more to Baskerville than to Caslon. Glasgow-based Alexander Wilson's type of the 1780s is robustly Baskervillean. Baskerville's own type and its punches eventually made their way to France following his death in 1775, and dropped from use in the nineteenth century. Revived in the early twentieth century, it has remained a staple ever since.

Although it still had it critics. Daniel Berkeley Updike, in *Printing Types* (1922), described Baskerville's first production, the Virgil of 1757, as 'Very easy to read, the volume nevertheless does not seem to me a particularly agreeable or *beautiful* book, partly on account of its type...' Francis Meynell, despite his praise, called the type 'a trifle finicky, a little too "correct"'. American designer Frederic Warde (*see* ARRIGHI) detected in it 'a quality of complacency which makes me think of a tombstone or a well-licked cat that has just died'. Bizarre imagery aside, Warde wasn't so wide of the mark in his first allusion. There is something monumental, with echoes of Roman inscriptions in stone, about Baskerville's title pages. It is Meynell's 'correctness' that gives the letters their distinctive aura, by no means an exaggerated description of their hypnotic and addictive effect on those to whom, aesthetically, they speak.

BODONI

FIRST APPEARANCE   ABOUT 1791, ITALY

DESIGNER   GIAMBATTISTA BODONI, ITALIAN

Bodoni is the most celebrated of the typefaces that fall into the category of 'Modern'. This category dates from the late eighteenth century and can trace its roots deep into the hinterland of the 1700s. Modern, in typographic terms, is defined by an extreme contrast in weight between thin and thick strokes. It formed part of a stylistic progression; Old Style essentially denotes a more even balance between thick and thin strokes, Transitional an increase in contrast, Modern pushing the thin strokes as far, in terms of satisfactory reproduction at text sizes, as they could go, while making the thick strokes thicker than before. It didn't stop there. For display, headline purposes, in the early nineteenth century the stroke weight imbalance was exponentially increased to create the Fat Face (*see* FAT FACE ITALIC)

On the Modern face, serifs are thin and flat, or almost flat, ideally meeting the upright stroke at a right angle. Stress – that is, where curved parts become thickest – is vertical, with the thinnest areas at the very top and bottom of the character. Modern typefaces have traditionally been most associated with the world of fashion, used for the title-pieces of magazines like *Vogue, Bazaar, Tatler*; if you picture the name Dior, it's likely your mind's eye has set it in a Modern letter. They have become visual shorthand for 'elegance', perhaps because of, in terms of form, their lack of grey areas. This part is thin, consistently thin, this thick and consistently so; here is a right angle, not a curve; upright in emphasis. The most elegant clothing is simple too, a man's evening clothes and 'the little black dress'. Perhaps also Modern types make a visual connection to the sparer style of fashion drawing of the later twentieth century, lines and splashes of colour, that moved away from the fuller illustrative styles of early-twentieth-century artists like George Barbier or André Marty, their figures placed in realistic settings.

However, the Modern faces have had their critics too. They became extremely dominant as book text faces in the nineteenth century, but require the careful presswork and a quality of paper that printers of the later 1800s, looking to maximize profits with high production runs to meet growing markets for the printed word, were not prepared to give. It was this deterioration in quality that was a spur for William Morris (*see* GOLDEN TYPE) to begin designing and printing with his own type. In the early decades of the twentieth century both Stanley Morison and Daniel Berkeley Updike, in his 1922 two-volume historical overview *Printing Types*, were both reproving of the popularity of the style and mildly censorious of its perpetrators. Morison, writing in *Four Centuries of Fine Printing* (1924) of the work of Giambattista Bodoni (1740–1813), accused him of having 'seduced every European typographer from allegiance to the more soundly built letters of obviously finer design known to printers as the "old faces"'. Updike described the Modern face as possessing 'rigid uniformity' that was mistaken for 'classic severity', and registered his qualified approval of 'Bodoni's great, chilly masterpieces, the *Oratio Dominica* and the *Manuale Tipografico*'.

Giambattista Bodoni was born in Saluzzo in Italy in 1740. The son of a printer, he was apprenticed in 1758 to the Propaganda Fide, the Vatican's printing house in Rome. His

MANUALE

TIPOGRAFICO

DEL CAVALIERE

GIAMBATTISTA BODONI

———

VOLUME PRIMO.

PARMA

·····❦·····

PRESSO LA VEDOVA

MDCCCXVIII.

'CHILLY MASTERPIECE': PAGES FROM BODONI'S *MANUALE TIPOGRAFICO*, 1818, COMPLETED BY HIS WIFE AFTER HIS DEATH.

LA VEDOVA BODONI

AL LETTORE.

⸺⸻◆⸻⸺

IL MANUALE TIPOGRAFICO, che
oggi presento al Pubblico, fa testi-
monianza amplissima delle grandi
cure che il mio diletto Consorte pose
all' incremento e perfezione dell' Arte
Tipografica. Dalla Prefazione che
lo precede, da lui scritta già da più
anni, e destinata a porsi in fronte
ai Saggi dell'industria, come egli

time there came to an end after eight years with the suicide of the director. Bodoni had seen and been excited by the work of John Baskerville (*see* BASKERVILLE), and, despite being unable to speak the language, decided to make his way to England. However, he contracted malaria en route, and returned to his parents' home to recover. It was while he was working in the family business that Ferdinando, the seventeen-year-old Duke of Parma, was persuaded by his prime minister, Guillaume Du Tillot, that the prestige of the duchy could be considerably magnified by the establishment of a royal press. Du Tillot and the duke wanted the duchy to be seen as a centre for arts and science, with a significant royal library. The recommendation of a former Roman connection of Bodoni's secured him the prestigious position of director at the royal printing house, where he was to stay for the rest of his life.

Du Tillot had become convinced of the need for a press capable of the highest quality work; previously, wanting to print a book to present to the incumbent duke's father, he had had to look outside the duchy to find craftsmen capable of the standards required. As well as acquiring paper and ink, he set the early typographic style of the press by buying type, elegant and Transitional in style, from the foundry of Pierre-Simon Fournier in Paris.

Bodoni worked prodigiously, and by the 1780s had made the ducal printing house one of the must-see stop-offs of a European Grand Tour. Baskerville's influence had spread as far as Italy with his 1773 edition of Ariosto's *Orlando Furioso*, printed in Italian and published there. Bodoni was surely influenced by his graphic style – wide margins, title pages with minimal ornament or pure type – although he was later to turn against his former inspiration, expressing a preference for Fournier and accusing Baskerville of – of all things – over-ornamentation.

The reputation of the press grew across Europe. Bodoni's development of his Modern face postdated that of Firmin Didot in France, between whom there was considerable professional jealousy, but in tandem they were responsible for the growth in the Modern style's popularity. By the beginning of the 1790s, Ferdinando, worried that Bodoni would be tempted by more attractive offers to leave Parma, allowed him to set up his own private press while still being in charge of the royal establishment. This gave Bodoni complete stylistic freedom, and the first book from the private press, Horace's *Flacci Opera* (1791), set the true Bodoni style – Modern type, often all upper case, letterspaced, minimal if any decoration, white space – a style which he would explore and perpetuate until his death.

Bodoni's work, like Baskerville's, is rarely if ever communicated in its full power in modern reproduction. As much as upon its own design, type and layout, it relied on the quality of the printing and of the materials used. His books have to be seen as actual artefacts to appreciate their full beauty. Then the effect is rarely less than stunning. Both Baskerville and Bodoni were craftsmen of artistic vision, who designed their books and printed them to exacting standards. In the hands of others, or in subsequent revivals, the outcomes can fall far short of this excellence. Bodoni as a typeface comes with not just a mood but a whole layout style in train, one of the factors that provoked the criticisms of Updike and Morison. But to adapt the statement of Updike, for 'classic severity' read simply 'classic'.

FAT FACE ITALIC

FIRST APPEARANCE   NINETEENTH CENTURY, BEFORE 1820,
GREAT BRITAIN
DESIGNER   UNKNOWN, ROBERT THORNE'S FOUNDRY, BRITISH

Early-nineteenth-century Britain saw a stylistic explosion of robust advertising display faces, the perfect typographic tools for facilitating the sale of the products of the Industrial Revolution. Although they have experienced periods of widescale revulsion, not least from Stanley Morison (*see* TIMES NEW ROMAN), who considered many of these faces to be the ugliest of all time, it is hard to look at most of them today without, at the very least, affection. One of these styles – and its very name invokes a feeling of bonhomie – was the Fat Face, which took Bodoni's ideal of high width contrast between thick and thin strokes, and pushed it to an absolute extreme. The contrast in the Fat Face was gargantuan, the perfect word to describe the bloated forms of the thick strokes, dwarfing into a comparative invisibility their etiolated counterparts.

Robert Thorne (1754–1820) is credited with a number of 'firsts': the first recorded examples of Modern typefaces, coiner of the term 'Egyptian' and the inventor of the Fat Face. Thorne had been an apprentice of Thomas Cottrell, a former apprentice of the Caslons, and later one of their rebel, secessionist employees. Cottrell died in 1785, and nine years later Thorne took over his foundry, merged it with his own and moved it from Nevil's Court in Fetter Lane first to no. 11 Barbican and then in 1808 to Fann Street, where it became the Fann Street Foundry. The last known Thorne type specimen

14 Line Pica, No. 2. Cast in Mould and Matrixes.

MAKER
Bardfield

A SHOWING OF A FAT FACE ITALIC BY WILLIAM THOROWGOOD IN HIS 1825
SPECIMEN BOOK.

dates from 1803, but he died in 1820 with a comfortable
fortune. From this, and from the fact that in 1819 he was
commissioned by France's Imprimerie Royale to cut them a
Fat Face, the only foreigner ever to receive a commission from
them, we can deduce that his was a successful business, both
financially and in terms of artistic reputation.

Following Thorne's death the Fann Street Foundry was
bought by William Thorowgood. He had no previous connection to typefounding or the graphic arts, having been the
London manager and agent for a patent roller pump business
based in Staffordshire. He is reputed to have bought Thorne's
foundry with the proceeds of a win on the state lottery.
However, he made a considerable success of his new profession,
becoming Letter-Founder to His Majesty in 1822. Although
he was to produce new faces of his own, his first specimens of
1820 and 1821 are almost entirely Robert Thorne's stock, which
gives us a useful insight into the unrecorded years of the latter's
foundry, and includes in numerous sizes the italic Fat Face.

Redolent though it is of late-Georgian and early- to mid-
Victorian England, in its largest sizes the italic reveals itself to

be akin in its design aesthetic to mid-1920s Bauhaus product design, its letterforms being based on straight lines and the curves of a near-circle. The thick stroke to thin stroke width ratio on the capitals is somewhat more than 25 to 1. The serifs are thin, square, unbracketed and stubby. Finials on some of the characters are outrageously obese, off-circular spots, by their sheer size forcing the upper case to become virtual swash characters. It is a design that is swaggering, ostentatious, unpretentious and brimming with warmth and good feeling. Despite the eventual fall from grace of the Fat Face and its contemporaries, by the mid-twentieth century they had rightly made some progress back into favour. The distinguished Ipswich-based printer W.S. Cowell offered Thorowgood's Fat Face Italic, 'probabl[y] … originally cut by Thorne', in its 1952 *A Book of Typefaces*, adding '[t]his recent revival is a most welcome addition to display faces'. The 1960s and 1970s would see a complete stylistic rehabilitation, with contemporary Fat Face or ultra weight designs enjoying popularity, such as Ed Benguiat's ITC Tiffany Heavy Italic, or the eponymous, self-explanatory 'Fat Face'.

TWO LINES
ENGLISH EGYPTIAN

FIRST APPEARANCE   1816, GREAT BRITAIN
DESIGNER   UNKNOWN, FOUNDRY OF WILLIAM CASLON IV,
BRITISH

In 1816 Caslon's foundry produced a new type specimen
which included a groundbreaking new entry: the first commercially available sans serif typeface, displayed with the words
W CASLON JUNR LETTERFOUNDER in capitals only, and in
one size. How popular it was at the time is hard to gauge, as
no immediately contemporary instances of its use are known,
although it remained on offer further into the nineteenth
century by the purchasers of Caslon's foundry. What prompted
its making, something of a stylistic and commercial leap in
the dark, is equally unknown, but there were precedents and a
growing cultural interest and awareness of sans serif, or at least
of monoline stroke lettering. Sans serif lettering was beginning
to feature in inscriptions, both celebratory and memorial, in
signwriting, and in the drawings of architects like Sir John
Soane.

The success of the Caslon foundry was built not on typographic innovation, but on the possession of a keen eye for the
demands of its market, and by meeting those needs with excellence. William I's Pica Roman drew heavily on existing models
currently being imported from mainland Europe, making
a superior product rather than a different one (*see* CASLON).
Subsequent internecine discord between William III and his

mother Elizabeth Caslon I, which led to the son breaking away to form his own foundry, are said to have been over the perceived conservatism of the original firm, a line of policy which, in the light of the maverick's subsequent bankruptcy, would have been seen to have been justified.

Surprisingly it was under the aegis of William Caslon IV (1780–1869) that the foundry produced its great innovation. Surprising, because the fourth Caslon was, of the Williams, least interested in typefounding – at least, he didn't regard it as a life's calling. He joined his father's reconstituted business in 1803, now one of two Caslon typefounding businesses. He took over the reins on William III's retirement in 1807, but in 1819 sold the company and devoted his efforts to a plan to illuminate London using coal gas. His work was recognized by the Society of Arts with a medal, but, having failed to patent his innovations, he received no financial benefit.

CANON ITALIC OPEN.

CUMBERLAND.

CANON ORNAMENTED.

TYPOGRAPHY.

TWO LINES ENGLISH EGYPTIAN.

W CASLON JUNR   LETTERFOUNDER

TWO LINES ENGLISH OPEN.

SALISBURY SQUARE.

CASLON'S GROUND-BREAKING SANS SERIF, MAKING ITS FIRST UNASSUMING APPEARANCE IN THE COMPANY'S 1816 SPECIMEN.

In the light of subsequent typographic nomenclature, Caslon's sans serif is confusing. Two Lines English referred to the type's physical size, double the size known as English, so equivalent to about 27 or 28 point. 'Egyptian' was a term later applied to slab serifs, type designs with large, angular, flat-topped and unbracketed serifs (*see* GUARDIAN EGYPTIAN).

But Egypt had been connected with what we would term a sans serif style since the beginning of the century. It had moved onto the cultural horizon for a section of the British public at the end of the eighteenth century as a result of the wars against the revolutionary French Republic. In 1798 Napoleon invaded Egypt, and in the same year Horatio Nelson defeated the French fleet in the Battle of the Nile. Napoleon, in one of those sophisticated initiatives that has made clear-cut analysis of his reputation and legacy a perpetually intriguing one for historians (*see* BRAILLE), took artists and scholars with his army to Egypt, with the aim of recording and analysing what they might find that was of historical and archaeological interest. Further French losses caused withdrawal from Egypt, and under the terms of the subsequent Treaty of Alexandria antiquities collected by the French were handed over to the victors. In this way Britain acquired the Rosetta Stone, uncovered by French engineers at el-Rashid. The stone bore a royal decree dating from 196 BCE, in three forms: Greek, Demotic (the everyday language of literate Egyptians) and hieroglyphics. The Stone provided the means of a breakthrough in the deciphering of hieroglyphics. Of secondary graphic interest was the style of the inscription of the Greek characters, in simple one-stroke incisions, the end result of which might be termed sans serif. Many would have seen the Stone, exhibited in 1802 in the British Museum (where it remains today), so the 'Egyptian' term of reference would have been widely understood.

THE PHYSICAL EXISTENCE OF A 'GHOST' TYPE, THE MATRICES OF TWO LINES
ENGLISH EGYPTIAN, PHOTOGRAPHED AT LONDON'S TYPE MUSEUM IN 2005.

Caslon's Two Lines English Egyptian is an unsophisticated
but solid face, its construction based on the square and the
circle. William Caslon IV's type was bought by Blake and
Garnett in 1819, and the Egyptian later featured in their
listings in the 1830s, but its use seems, so far as is known, to
have been limited. Although nineteenth-century sans serifs,
or grotesques as they came to be known, can be regarded as
crude in comparison to the sophistication brought to the form
by designers like Edward Johnston and Paul Renner, many
have an uncalculating energy and charm that designers in the
smoother, polished age of digital type design have sometimes
sought to recapture. Two Lines English Egyptian has that
quality, and was revived in 2000 for the signage for Dulwich
Picture Gallery in South London, one of sans serif pioneer-user
Sir John Soane's finest architectural treasures.

POUCHÉE'S 18 LINES NO. 2

FIRST APPEARANCE 1820S, GREAT BRITAIN

DESIGNER UNKNOWN, FOUNDRY OF LOUIS JOHN POUCHÉE, PROBABLY FRENCH

[A]lthough only FOUR Type Foundries (exclusive of mine) are worked in London at this time, the jealousy of those who have had so long possession of the Trade, would in its tenacious operation (as manifested in their treatment of me), seem to bespeak that they consider themselves EXCLUSIVELY entitled to all its advantages, 'AD INFINITUM'...

Of the Specimens which I shall have the Honour to submit to your notice in the progress of the Concern, I will be bold to state, with the facilities I have ensured, by an employment of the best Talent in every Branch, that they will shew my Types to be at least equal to any that have preceded them.

Address to the Printers, L.J. Pouchée,
New Type Foundry, Great Wild-Street, London, 1819

Type design and printing, although their objective may sometimes have been the achievement of beauty, have always been, as Gutenberg knew so well, a business. And few can have lambasted his business competitors, and enraged them so much, as Louis John Pouchée (*c.* 1782–1845). His name would suggest he was at least of French ancestry, and his presence is first recorded in London in 1810. Careerwise, he had more than one string to his bow, running a restaurant in Holborn and also working – for a while concurrently – as a coal merchant. It was probably also during this period that he established his type foundry.

His earliest known type specimen, from 1819, offered an unremarkable array of type styles from the period, but beyond

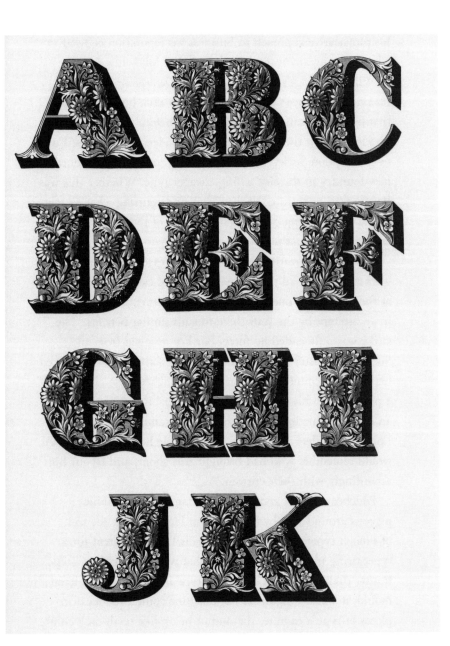

LOUIS JOHN POUCHÉE'S 18 LINES NO. 2, SUPERLATIVE ARTISTRY BY
AN UNKNOWN ARTIST.

his provocative approach to business his reputation is owed to what his company was to produce in the following decade.

William Savage's *Practical Hints on Decorative Printing* of 1822 dates Pouchée's establishment from 1818, but it is possible that he was operating in the field even before that date. An 1812 letter from the Edinburgh typefounder Alexander Wilson to the London Society of Master Letter Founders mentioned a new foundry in the city selling cheaper type. Whether this was Pouchée's is open to conjecture, but undercutting what he saw as the overcharging of his rivals was one of the planks of his combative business policy.

Another provocative move was to increase the wages of his workmen. This had the dramatic effect of causing a strike at the foundry of one of his great competitors, Edmund Fry, in an attempt by the staff there to gain similar benefits. The strike was only ended by force, but Fry resigned from the Society of Master Letter Founders amid acrimony, and reduced his prices to counter the threat from Pouchée, who claimed in a postscript to his 'Address to the Printers' that he had forced an overall reduction in the price of type among the other London founders of about 12 per cent. He hoped the printers would remember who had brought this about, and favour him accordingly with their custom.

Pouchée released another cat among the typographic pigeons around 1823 by buying from Henri Didot, the son of French typefounder Pierre-François Didot, a patent for a typecasting machine, producing what was called polyamatype. Rather than casting each piece of type individually in a hand mould, it was claimed that the machine could produce 400 pieces of type a minute, the output being like teeth on a comb. The individual pieces of type were then broken off a central strip of lead. Even if in practice the machine fell short of this total, it still meant that Pouchée could produce his type at a radically cheaper cost than his competitors.

When Pouchée decided to end his foundry in 1830, the feelings of his one-time rivals, now potential customers for the purchase of all his equipment and effects, made themselves known. Pouchée ended up melting down much of his type rather than sell it at prices he considered insulting. One probable successful sale was the polyamatype machine, about whose fate three different stories circulated. The first was that Pouchée's own workmen had destroyed it, because it didn't work; the second was that it was bought by Caslon & Livermore, who transported it to their premises and carried out a similar act of destruction. The third, and perhaps most appealing, claimed that a group of Pouchée's fellow founders clubbed together to buy it, towed it out to sea and consigned it to the depths. Pouchée, ever the Renaissance man, later ran a tollbooth on the outskirts of London.

It seems likely that, polyamatype machine or not, a purchase was made by Caslon at the closing-down sale. In 1936, at another closing-down sale, this time of H.W. Caslon, the type company Monotype bought twenty-three alphabets of wooden letters, which had been engraved on boxwood. Thought at one point to have been reduced to ashes by the bomb that destroyed Monotype's London headquarters in 1941, they were later rediscovered and given to Oxford University Press, then to London's St Bride Library. Only since the 1990s has their provenance been confirmed as being of Pouchée's foundry. So intricate was their production that it is unlikely that they would have been mass-produced, but rather would have been intended as moulds from which castings could be made in type metal that could then be mounted on wooden blocks to the required height for printing. They are in varying large sizes, intended for display type and poster work.

The basic type style for most of the alphabets is of three-dimensional fat faces, an extreme version of the Modern type style with emaciated thin strokes and gargantuan heavy ones, a very fashionable style at that time, which had the physical advantage of presenting large stroke areas on which to carry ornament. Pouchée's foundry had earned its inclusion in Savage's book through 'a variety of Ornamental Letters ... looked on as peculiarly applicable where the subject is conviviality, masonry, or music', and the Pouchée letters follow a variety of illustrative themes, including music, fruit, acorns, sunburst flowers, masonic symbols (Pouchée himself was a freemason) and agricultural animals and equipment. They look to be the work of different artists. Some are more simply graphic in style; a small number, such as the one known as 18 Lines No. 2, are far more sophisticated.

18 Lines No. 2 is essentially a three-dimensional fat face, with thin, flat serifs. Its sides, representing the third dimension, are simple black. The body of the letter bears a lightly striated pattern. But upon that, seemingly growing both on and out of the letterform, and sometimes creating organic serifs, are leaves and flowers, so skilfully rendered as to give the effect of fine engraving. In addition to the basic *tromp l'œil* of the three-dimensional letterform, the engraver's use of light and shade gives the striking effect of a second physical level of malleable yet solid natural forms; the type seems almost to burst off the page. In places, bifurcated finials are created by the device of two leaves with a central bud.

Who the creators of Pouchée's designs were is unknown. Similarly unclear is how successful the alphabets were in commercial terms. Was it financial failure or just a loss of enthusiasm for the business that caused Pouchée to sell up in 1830? The decorated alphabets' intended use would have been in advertising and display, but such items are ephemera, and do not survive in the numbers that books do, so from this distance of time it is impossible to gauge their popularity.

Pouchée boasted that his higher wages bought him a comparable standard of artisan. Perhaps it was indeed this policy that resulted in such a startling divergence from the foundry's more workaday offerings, and that securing the services of the best craftsmen available made it possible to produce such visually opulent alphabets, 'at least equal to any that have preceded them'.

BRAILLE

FIRST APPEARANCE   1820S, FRANCE
DESIGNER   LOUIS BRAILLE, FRENCH

If the entries in this book were graded like a top 50, the no. 1
position would probably have to go to Gutenberg's type for
the 42-line Bible, because it made everything else possible. But
behind it in second place, and standing outside all the other
entries' terms of reference, must be braille. Beyond its untold
benefits to visually impaired people, graphically and conceptually it represents a startlingly modernistic modular system.
Although braille's visual appearance is irrelevant, the beauty
and simplicity of its design is what makes it work. It was the
work of a person only in their early teens. But it was probably
because of Louis Braille's extreme youth, and because he had
lost his sight so young, that he was able to apply thought
processes untrammelled or sidetracked by previous experience.

Born in Coupvray near Paris in 1809, Louis Braille blinded
himself in one eye at the age of three playing with the tools
in his father's workshop. Infection spread to the other eye
and by five he was completely blind. His parents nonetheless
encouraged him to overcome his disability and to proceed with
his education. Aged ten he went to one of the first schools for
the blind in Paris, the Royal Institute for Blind Youth. The
school's founder Valentin Haüy had devised a reading system
based on the embossed impressions of roman characters. The
books were few, cumbersome and expensive to produce; the
school's library only had fourteen copies. Reading was a slow
process, and once the pupils left the school there was little

ORIENTAL BRAILLE FOR THE BLIND.

अ आ इ ई उ ऊ ऋ ( ) ए ऐ ( ) औ औ

a ā i ī u ū ri e ē ai o ō au ṃ ḥ

क ख ग घ ङ	Palatals	च छ ज झ ञ	Cerebrals	ट ठ ड ढ ण
k kh g gh ṅ		ć ćh j jh ñ		ṭ ṭh ḍ ḍh ṇ
त थ द ध न	Labials	प फ ब भ म	Semi-vowels	य र ल व
t th d dh n		p ph b bh m		y r l w
श ष स ह ळ	NUMBERS	Prefix १ २ ३ ४ ५ ६ ७ ८ ९ ०		
ś ṣ s h !		1 2 3 4 5 6 7 8 9 0		

Remainder the 63 Signs: ā ū ē ŏ (aw ° r r zh z q x

CHRISTIAN LITERATURE SOCIETY FOR INDIA,
55, John Street, Bedford Row, London. W.C.

A CARD OF UNKNOWN DATE SHOWING BRAILLE PRODUCED BY THE CHRISTIAN LITERATURE SOCIETY FOR INDIA.

likelihood they would encounter embossed books in the world outside. Braille felt that, although the concept of reading by touch was the right direction, a better system could be devised.

The germ of Braille's idea came from elsewhere, however; its original spark of inspiration is traceable to that great creator of systems and, in his day job, re-creator of national boundaries – Napoleon Bonaparte. In 1821 a demonstration took place at the school by Charles Barbier, a French army captain. Barbier's

Please Touch

CONTEMPORARY MUSEUM SIGNAGE, NEWCASTLE-UPON-TYNE, ENGLAND.

system was called *écriture nocturne*, night-writing, developed in response to Bonaparte's request for a means for soldiers to exchange messages in darkness soundlessly and without light. Barbier used raised dots for his letters on a grid of two columns of six possible dot positions. These corresponded to the horizontal and vertical coordinates of a larger 36-position grid, which featured both single letters and common combinations. It had proved too difficult for troops to grasp, and had been abandoned. Although Braille was able to master it, most of his fellow students gave up the attempt. A major problem was that many of the dot combinations were, because of the structure of Barbier's grid, spread over too large an area on the page to be read by a single touch of the fingertip.

Braille simplified the grid to two columns of three – apparently much to Barbier's umbrage at his system being overhauled by one so young – and presented his first workable version aged only fifteen. Originally the Braille system worked on a letter-by-letter basis, but later modifications used contractions, as Barbier's had, akin to shorthand. Braille eventually created sixty-three characters, including punctuation and common words, and later musical notation and mathematical symbols. In 1829 he published his prospectus for the system,

Method of Writing Words, Music and Plain Songs by Means of Dots, for Use by the Blind and Arranged for Them.

Braille was able to demonstrate his breakthrough at the 1834 Paris Exposition of Industry, but although apparently attracting the attention of the minister of the interior in the company of the French king, Louis-Philippe, no action was taken to bring his innovations to the wider world. Even the Institute, where Braille had stayed on as a teacher, eventually abandoned the use of braille, seeing it as setting the blind apart from the sighted by giving them their own dedicated, tailor-made tool for understanding and communication. Braille was not adopted by the school until two years after its creator's early death in 1852.

Braille's wasn't the only touch-based reading system created in the first half of the nineteenth century. A near-contemporary system was developed in Britain, the Moon alphabet, devised by William Moon (1818–1894). Moon had lost the sight of one eye through scarlet fever at the age of four, becoming completely blind at twenty-one. His twenty-six letters were presented by nine shapes, some rotated at 90-degree angles to give four different possible letters. There were also numerals, punctuation and word-ending combinations, 'ing', 'ment', 'tion' and 'ness'. The Moon alphabet first appeared in 1845. John Rutherfurd's *William Moon and his Work for the Blind* (1898) states that at the time of writing more than 20,000 people in the United Kingdom had learned to read using the Moon system. Although less well known than Braille's system, Moon has advantages for very old and very young learners, and also those with a less developed sense of touch. Its characters are larger, and most bear a structural relation to the roman character forms. It was produced as metal type by Monotype and other typefounders in the twentieth century, and digital software now plays a part in its generation.

The English and Chinese ADVERTISER.

PRINTED AND PUBLISHt BY ROBERT BELL, MAIN ROAD, BALLAARAT

帖 招 唇 英

2ND. YEAR – NO. 60   SATURDAY NOVEMBER 28 1857.   GRATIS

V.   R.
GOVERNMENT   NOTICE.

The following regulations, drawn up by the Chinese Protector of the District, will be given to the Headman of each Village, whose duty it will be to see them duly enforced, under a Penalty of £5, or Two Months Imprisonment.

All Tents must be pitched in a straight line and face the same way, with an Interval of not less than 3 Feet, between Each. Proper space must be preserved for streets, and no encroachments will be allowed upon them. These streets where it is practible will be 25 Feet Wide.

The Inhabitants of each Tent will have to keep a can free from rubbish the immediate neighbourhood of the same. no Slaughter Yards, sheep Folds, &c., will be allowed inside the Village.

Obedience must be given in all respects to the head men, but should it be supposed that they abuse their authority by insisting upon that which they have no right to demand, it is requested that immediate information be given to the Protector, who will enquire into the matter.

諭 告 家 皇

為曉諭事爾等圜人知悉前出所立之規條
皆託各方管事之人支辦倘若管事之人
不能要當照例罰民五榜但凡事務圜人
爾等照例而行或有特頑不遵照例重責

凡搭布帳門口全向至少離三尺

凡街巷大路留餘地二十五尺方可蓋搭

凡各人所居之地方布帳門口要潔淨

凡各人所居之地方勿搭豬羊欄在街內

一千八百五十七年七月四日

WM HENRY FOSTER, CHINESE PROTECTOR,

AN 1857 EDITION OF ROBERT BELL'S FREE NEWSPAPER.

CHINESE ADVERTISER
CHARACTERS

FIRST APPEARANCE 1856, AUSTRALIA
DESIGNER ROBERT BELL, BRITISH/AUSTRALIAN,
WITH UNKNOWN CONTRIBUTORS

On 12 February 1851, gold was discovered in New South
Wales, Australia. Later, richer fields were found at Ballarat and
Bendigo in Victoria, and the Australian Gold Rush was on,
only three years after its more celebrated Californian predecessor. Melbourne and Ballarat were unable to accommodate the
enormous influx of prospectors, and tent cities grew on their
outskirts, rapidly turning to slums. In ten years the population of Victoria increased by nearly 600 per cent. Its Chinese
population rose from a little under 2,500 in 1854 to over 25,000
in 1857, and reached an estimated, albeit temporary, high of
42,000 in 1859. A small number of these would have pre-dated
the gold rush, the gradual ending by the British of the policy
of transportation of convicted criminals having created a need
for cheap labour. However, most would have arrived in search
of their fortunes, many from Guangdong province, escaping
upheavals and repression in their own country.

The British Empire's relations with China during this
period were fraught, with the two Opium Wars of 1839–1842
and 1856–1860 being fought by the British, and later the
French, to open up China to trade on British terms. Such an
influx of Chinese into Australia was regarded at best with
suspicion, an unease that the racial composition of the country

would be undesirably compromised. At worst they were seen as a threat to security, capable of rising en masse to impose Chinese control on Australia, despite the large majority of the new arrivals being economic migrants and refugees from sometimes renewed persecution. The result was prejudice, taxation and sometimes persecution. Chinese miners with established claims often lost them to Europeans through their inability to pay the separate, higher taxes levied upon them.

Little is known of Robert Bell, the publisher of *The Chinese Advertiser*. He was born in Middlesex, England, and died in poverty in Ballarat in 1905 aged eighty-eight, after having collapsed in his 'hovel' and being taken to the infirmary. He was buried in an unmarked grave, but the passing of 'Chinese Bell' did merit notice in some newspapers. It was recorded that he had studied chemistry, botany, medicine and surgery at University College, London in the 1830s, and had arrived in Victoria in 1852. There is no record of his arrival by ship in the colony, but he may have landed elsewhere in Australia and made his way overland. His study of the Chinese language is thought to have begun at this point. In April 1856 the *Ballarat Star* announced that the town was 'to have a third [news-paper], which speaks more than ever of our energy, and public spirit; it will be the organ of our Chinese population, and be printed in Chinese characters'. The first issue of *The Chinese Advertiser* appeared in mid-April or early May 1856. As well as translations of official notices, it contained 'extracts from Chinese Composition, and the Scriptures'. The paper was sub-titled 'Pioneer of Christianity and Christian civilisation among the Chinese in Australasia'. Contributions were accepted from Chinese missionaries, and Bell offered to print small items such as handbills in Chinese. In a September 1857 letter to Sir Henry Barkly, the governor of Victoria, Bell informed him that he was able to feature government announcements in 'the better sort of Chinese Writing'.

In 1857 the newspaper was renamed *The English and Chinese Advertiser*, and was published in both languages, weekly, in a single-sheet, four-page format. It was distributed free of charge on Saturdays to the Chinese villages, the tent cities, on the outskirts of the town, and was recognized sufficiently to be included among the items placed in the cavity of the foundation stone of the Ballarat Miners' Exchange in October 1857.

A long-running advertisement in the newspaper was for wood for making coffins, a testament to the high mortality rate among the Chinese in the goldfields. There are other clear indicators of the hardships and threats the Chinese had to endure. One advertisement stated: 'The theatre has a new show, Chinese are welcome to see. If westerners make trouble, the pub will manage.' Elsewhere a government notice warned that if the Chinese prospectors did not maintain their licence payments 'the officials will not intervene in any problems Chinese diggers face, including being bullied by westerners'. Instruction was also given to the Chinese through the newspaper to help them to count in English, to assist them in understanding and achieving fair transactions.

Bell was journalist, editor and the printer of the *Advertiser*, but whether his duties included designer and typographer is uncertain. His Chinese characters, on the evidence of surviving issues of the newspaper, vary from probable bronze castings to cruder examples presumed to have been cut from wood by Bell himself. But in later issues there is a marked improvement in quality, using two different styles of Chinese calligraphy, so it seems probable that Bell was able to recruit Chinese craftsmen to make woodblocks of the characters.

There is uncertainty about how long *The English and Chinese Advertiser* lasted; dating by commentators ranges from 1858 to late 1860. The Chinese population in Ballarat decreased dramatically during 1858–59. With the subsequent ending of the colony's Chinese Protectorate, with its officials responsible for collecting taxes, interpreting and administering relations between the communities, loss of the revenue and editorial authority from the government notices formerly published may well have dealt a death blow to the paper.

As well as publishing the *Advertiser*, Bell wrote articles for English-language newspapers defending the interests of the Chinese. He wanted to set up a school for the Chinese, and continued to argue for justice and understanding on their behalf in the face of continuing prejudice, which later manifested itself in one of the first pieces of legislation passed by the new Australian Federation in 1901, the Immigration Restriction Act. The Australian prime minister Edmund Barton asserted that the idea of the equality of man was never meant to apply to the Chinese.

What made Bell see things differently? He was able to see the Chinese in Australia as fellow human beings rather than aliens, and he and his newspaper represented a remarkable if brief flowering, evidence of a finer human spirit than that possessed by most with whom he came into confrontation. Ballarat experienced far less antagonism between the communities than at other diggings. Perhaps the efforts of Bell and the existence of *The Chinese and English Advertiser* were a contributing factor to this comparative harmony.

FRENCH ANTIQUE

FIRST APPEARANCE   ABOUT 1854, GREAT BRITAIN
DESIGNER   UNKNOWN, FOUNDRY OF ROBERT BESLEY, BRITISH

The allure of the American Wild West reached its peak during
the golden age of Hollywood, the 1930s through to the 1950s.
It swept into television in the following decade, was given a
memorable, convulsive twist through Italian and internation-
ally financed 'spaghetti westerns', then petered out in the 1970s.
There are occasional small-scale revivals of interest, usually featuring a reworking of one or more genre stereotypes. Although
during this time there was an accompanying thematic thread
in popular or pulp fiction, the genre was most effective as a
visual one, thriving on what swiftly became clichés, but no less
effective because of that: good or evil indicated by the colour of
a stetson; confrontational gunslingers on a deserted main street
of a one-horse town, hands twitching above pearl-handled
six-shooters; treacherous, bestubbled Mexicans concealing
bowie knives under the shadow of sombreros; the love interest
from the east, whose soft hands are willing by the end of the
film to tear a strip off her expensive gown to bandage the hero;
the six-note sequence that always denoted 'Indians!' as they
appeared in a line on the crest of a hill; the stagecoach racing
across Monument Valley with 'redskins' in hot pursuit.

It is of course history written by the winners; the realization
of the United States' concept of 'manifest destiny' to justify
what was in essence an imperialist expansion to rival that of
any nineteenth-century European power, with an accompanying clearance of Native Americans and the irksome presence of

Mexico. But as a mythology, and a form of entertainment, in its time the Wild West has proven irresistible.

A graphic element in its intensely wrought physical landscape was the poster tacked to the wooden walls of buildings in frontier towns, headed by the single word 'Wanted', usually above a pictorial representation of an outlaw, a cold-blooded killer with a price on his head. Typographically the lettering would be in a style that has come to be known as 'Wild West';

FORTY LINE FRENCH ANTIQUE ELONGATED, 7s. 6d. PER DOZ.

TWENTY-FIVE LINE FRENCH ANTIQUE ELONGATED, 4s. 9d. PER DOZ.

DAY & COLLINS, ATLAS WORKS, LONDON, E.C.

A NINETEENTH-CENTURY SHOWING FROM DAY & COLLINS'S *SPECIMENS OF WOOD TYPE* OF 1880; OPPOSITE, EVOKING THE WILD WEST FOR NOEL COWARD'S PERFORMANCE IN LAS VEGAS, 1966.

highly condensed, with top and bottom serifs, strokes, and sections of curves within the upper and lower quarters of the cap height extremely fat. Strokes within the central two quarters were thin and monoline.

The style, although strongly associated with frontier America, was originally called French Antique, and more confusingly was produced first in England in the mid-1850s by the Fann Street Letter Foundry, now run by Robert Besley. It was in essence a more sophisticated development of a style that had appeared in the early 1820s, the Italian. The style concept of the Italian was to reverse the weight of thick and thin strokes, and the thick and thin sections of curves. As a style it had its critics, both contemporary and of the early twentieth century, when such attention-grabbing nineteenth-century advertising faces were largely reviled. The French Antique kept the spirit of the concept but imposed some spatial organization, resulting in a design that was easier on the eye. An intermediate stop on the design trajectory was the Clarendon, of which condensed examples, with similar vertical distributions of weight, pre-date by a few years the appearance in the United States of French Antique. Clarendons differed in that the serifs were bracketed, curved, while those of the French Antiques were unbracketed, meeting the stroke at a right angle.

The first known record of the design in the United States is credited to William H. Page & Co. in 1869. William Hamilton

Page (1829–1909) founded his company in Norwich, Connecticut, and it became a major manufacturer of wood type until he sold the business in 1891 to his rival, the Hamilton Manufacturing Company. Page's design appeared in James Conner's Sons' *Typographic Messenger*, of July 1869. The style was quickly poached by his competitors and remained extremely popular until the 1890s, when it fell quite sharply from favour – possibly a side effect of the William Morris-inspired Arts and Crafts influence making itself felt in the United States (*see* GOLDEN TYPE). Whatever the truth of its prevalence as suggested by Hollywood, the French Antique's appearance and decline coincide almost exactly with the period of western expansion.

Some decades later on the other side of the Atlantic, Sheffield-based typefounders Stephenson Blake flew in the face of prevailing typographic tastes by releasing Robert Harling's Playbill in 1938. Again it was a prescient move, although they may have had to wait for the face to achieve popularity. But the late 1940s and early 1950s saw a revival of what were seen as thoroughly British faces. Ipswich printers W.S. Cowell in their beautiful 1952 specimen *A Book of Typefaces* said of Playbill: 'This Stephenson Blake revival of French Antique has been very popular … it is effective in pastiche Victorian settings and perhaps even more so – through surprising contrast with its surroundings – in a thoroughly contemporary arrangement.'

Faces catering for the style were always available in the photosetting era, either Playbill itself, or derivatives under different names, such as Old Town or Boots and Saddles. The era of American wooden poster types has seen a revival in the twenty-first century with numerous faces in the collection of Wisconsin's Hamilton Wood Type and Printing Museum being made available as digital fonts.

TYPEWRITER FACES

FIRST APPEARANCE   LATE NINETEENTH CENTURY, USA

For people born before about 1975, or even a little later, their first experience of creating written language using something other than their own handwriting would have been with a typewriter. And it was an exciting experience to see your own words transformed by a medium that transported them into another realm – adult, professional, believable. Portable in the later lighter models, cheap at entry level, the typewriter had been an essential business tool of the twentieth century, and is still of use in parts of the world where a steady electrical supply cannot be relied upon.

Like type itself, the invention of the typewriter has numerous candidates, by one tally as many as 112. Once moveable type was an established form of communication in Europe, it would take no great leap of imagination to speculate whether the idea of the reversed image of a character cast in metal, coated with ink and coming into contact with paper, could have a further application. But for inventions to flourish there has to be a demand or a need. Some nineteenth-century inventors saw one benefit of their writing machines as being for the blind (*see* BRAILLE): Celestino Galli's Potenografo, reported in *The Times* in 1831, although possibly never actually built, was one example. Both Pierre Foucault, himself blind, and G.A. Hughes won medals at London's 1851 Great Exhibition for their machines. Hughes was the director of the Henshaw Institute for the Blind in Manchester; his 'Typograph' created embossed characters.

But it was the increasing pace of business in the nineteenth century, stoked by the mechanization of the Industrial Revolution, that created the need for a communication tool that could generate words faster than the speed of human handwriting, and with the added bonus of being always legible. The first successful, commercially produced typewriter is credited for the bulk of its development work in the late 1860s to Christopher Latham Sholes and Carlos Glidden. E. Remington and Sons, who had begun in 1816 as a firearm maker in upstate New York, had by this point branched out into sewing machines and farming equipment, and acquired the rights to put the machine into production in 1873. The first model had only upper-case letters, but used a QWERTY keyboard layout largely similar to the one still in use today. The second Remington model of 1878 introduced the use of lower-case letters.

In terms of social impact, the typewriter is credited with giving women, with their forced acceptance of lower wages, opportunities to move from factory work into the world of the office. So prevalent were the machines by the late nineteenth century that Sherlock Holmes, who would later, in *The Hound of the Baskervilles*, also instruct Watson in the individuality of newspaper typefaces, was able to offer observations in *A Case of Identity* (1891) on the nature of typescript: 'a typewriter has really quite as much individuality as a man's handwriting. Unless they are quite new, no two of them write exactly alike.' This individuality is a plot device that has been exploited in crime fiction and film many times since.

By the late 1890s American Type Founders were offered a typewriter face, a stylistic range that they developed over the next quarter of a century, even creating faces to match the output of the models of particular manufacturers such as Smith-Premier, a popular machine since 1890.

Anna Freud
Normality and Pathology
in Childhood

DIRECT AND
UNPRETENTIOUS:
A TYPEWRITER FACE
ON ANNA FREUD'S
*NORMALITY AND
PATHOLOGY IN
CHILDHOOD*, DESIGNED
BY JOHN MCCONNELL,
1973.

This desire, or market, to create type to imitate the appearance of what was in effect the printed word's poorer relation, the typewritten word – itself trying to imitate the clarity of text produced by a printer – was an interesting circular reference, doubly so in that it appeared so soon. ATF in their 1923 specimen book set up a sample page of 12-point New Model Smith-Premier Typewriter, and explained: 'Imitation typewritten letters have come to occupy an important place in the industrial world of today ... Many offices have found the production of imitation typewritten letters very profitable...' ATF went on to elaborate how, for added verisimilitude, their face was designed to be printed through 'silk, crepe chiffon or regular ribbon cloth' to lose that crispness of impression that properly printed letterpress had, and that a typewritten character lacked.

The classic typewriter alphabet was both monoline and monospaced, each character occupying an identical width space on the page, the typewriter's 'invisible grid'. It is squarish, with a large x-height. The serifs are also monoline, characteristically with a slight 'blob', a rounded thickening at its end, pronounced on the descenders of the p, q and y, and at the top of the l and the j. Clarity and distinctiveness of character are paramount. They are monoline because the inescapable variability of impression, dependent on the quality and age of the typewriter ribbon, which held the ink, and the weight contained in the strike of the finger on the key, didn't favour subtleties of stroke weight.

Digital typewriter fonts such as Courier have always been present as standard system fonts. So synonymous were the images of the characters with one-to-one written communication that in the early years of the personal computer it felt strange, and visually confusing, to write a letter using what were traditionally typefaces for print.

Typewriter faces are at once utilitarian and romantic, everyday and mysterious, impersonal and threatening. Use one in a design and it can suggest espionage, secret government agencies working for good or evil, or the grey areas in between. The Third Reich's most cataclysmic, genocidal decisions would have been disseminated in typewriter script, the 'banality of evil' encapsulated. Impersonal, yet, as Holmes pointed out, with a personality nonetheless. This perceived impersonality was such that, in the pre-digital age, it was long considered discourteous to type a personal letter. But, despite this, the typewriter style carries as much cultural baggage as Fraktur.

GOLDEN TYPE

FIRST APPEARANCE 1891, GREAT BRITAIN
DESIGNERS WILLIAM MORRIS AND EMERY WALKER, BRITISH

Ask most people today what the name William Morris means to them, and the response, if any, would probably be 'wallpaper'. It's a correct answer, of course, but barely scratches the surface of a complex personality and life. Morris, Marshall, Faulkner & Company, later Morris & Company – a brand name still in use today – were responsible, following the company's inception in 1861, for several enduring designs in the field of wall coverings, rich and densely wrought visions of foliage, flowers and birds, an aesthetic that extended to much of the furniture and fabrics they designed and marketed for the complete Morris interior. Novelist, ardent socialist, political campaigner and writer, publisher, printer and type designer, initially Morris was most remembered following his death in 1896 as a poet.

It is to him that we owe the idea of a design philosophy, of developing an aesthetic based on a logical system of thought or beliefs, and applying it to every aspect of life. 'Have nothing in your home that you do not know to be useful, or believe to be beautiful' is probably his best-known quotation. This was a man who, in his teenage years, found it impossible to visit the 1851 Great Exhibition, so appalled was he by the prospect of the over-elaborate, conceptually nonsensical room clutter that represented much of mid-Victorian design. His work and his ideas became inspirational; some adopted them wholeheartedly while others drew upon them to develop their own philosophies. His influence spread from Britain to the United States and to mainland Europe. As just one major example of his reach, the Bauhaus in Germany would not have developed in the way it did, or possibly even existed at all, without Morris and his ideas of the maintenance of the standards of craftsmanship in a machine age, the status and importance of the artist/craftsman, and of ordinary men and women.

Born in Walthamstow in 1834, Morris came late to publishing and printing. Although he had shown some interest in letterforms before this date, type history pinpoints his moment of revelation as a lecture, with lantern slides, given by Emery Walker at the first exhibition of the Arts and Crafts Society in Regent Street, London, in 1888. Walker (1851–1933) was a near neighbour of Morris's in Hammersmith, and a fellow socialist, working alongside him as secretary in successive organizations. Walker's schooling terminated when he was aged about twelve owing to his father's blindness and the need to provide financially to support his family. Walker was largely, and voraciously, self-educated, and ended his life with a knighthood. His company specialized in graphic reproduction; he was expert in engraving processes and the high-quality reproduction of photographs and illustrations. Although Morris wrote afterwards that the nervous Walker could have helped himself by preparing some notes for the talk, he found electrifying the photographic enlargements of typefaces shown, and had already determined on the way home to start his own publishing venture.

Morris was a man at odds with his age; he felt that the Victorian focus on mass production to achieve maximum profit was destroying quality and crushing the working life and very existence of the craftsman. Whatever its shortcomings, he looked back to the Middle Ages as an ordered society

CHAPTER XV. YET HALLBLITHE SPEAKETH WITH THE KING.

O wore the days & the moons; and now were some six moons worn since first he came to the Glittering Plain; & he was come to Wood-end again, and heard & knew that the King was sitting once more in the door of his pavilion to hearken to the words of his people, and he said to himself: "I will speak yet again to this man, if indeed he be a man; yea, though he turn me into stone." ❡ And he went up toward the pavilion; and on the way it came into his mind what the men of the kindred were doing that morning; and he had a vision of them as it were, and saw them yoking the oxen to the plough, and slowly going down the acres, as the shining iron drew the long furrow down the stubble-land, and the light haze hung about the elm-trees in the calm morning, and the smoke rose straight into the air from the roof of the kindred. And he said: "What is this? am I death-doomed this morning that this sight cometh so clearly upon me amidst the falseness of this unchanging land?"

❡ Thus he came to the pavilion, and folk fell

101

THE FIRST BOOK PRINTED BY MORRIS'S KELMSCOTT PRESS:
THE STORY OF THE GLITTERING PLAIN, 1891.

in which the artist and craftsman had a place and that most valuable commodity, time, at his disposal. One area in which this loss of quality was very apparent was in printing and typography. Much nineteenth-century text was printed in debased versions of Modern-style type, with high contrast thick and thin strokes. Printed without care on low-quality paper, the impressions of the characters would break up, to the detriment of both the page's aesthetic appearance and the reading experience. With Britain's dramatically expanding nineteenth-century population and, following the 1870 Education Act, a growth in literacy, there was an increase in demand and a growing market for newspapers, popular magazines and books. Speed and volume in production took precedence over quality.

So when Morris came to consider the nature of the books of what would become the Kelmscott Press, he deemed it essential that he design his own type. It was here that Walker, although declining a partnership in the Press – possibly foreseeing that Morris would dominate proceedings in any such relationship – was crucial as a consultant and collaborator. Morris wanted 'letter pure in form; severe, without needless excrescences; solid, without the thickening and thinning of the line, which is the essential fault of ordinary modern type, and which makes it difficult to read; and not compressed laterally, as all later type has grown to be owing to commercial exigencies'. Despite his aversion to machine production and many of the trappings of modernity, his type was realized through the very modern medium of photography. Walker photographed and enlarged pages from two fifteenth-century sources, Nicolas Jenson's Italian edition of Pliny's *Historia Naturalis* and Jacobus Rubeus's edition of Leonardo Bruni's *Historia Fiorentina*, both published in 1476. From these images drawings were made for the new type. The punches were cut by Edward Prince, who went on to perform the same service for most of the significant British typefaces of the private press movement that Morris inspired. Following Morris's lead, no self-respecting private press could have any pretension to be taken seriously without its own custom typeface.

Morris had intended the Kelmscott Press's first production to be an edition of Jacobus de Voragine's *The Golden Legend*, but with delays in paper deliveries it was decided to switch to a shorter alternative, a reprint of Morris's own *The Story of the Glittering Plain*. This was also the first showing of the new type, christened Golden in honour of the original scheme.

The visual effect of the Kelmscott Press books has been described as 'the black page' as opposed to the twentieth century's 'grey page'. The original edition of *The Story of the Glittering Plain* was relatively simple in its design, but subsequent publications featured intensely illustrated and decorated pages, in Morris & Company style. But the visual weight of the page was considerably increased by the type. Generous of x-height, it was, as Morris wished, without great contrast in stroke weight. In creating the drawings, account would have had to be taken of the spread of ink on the original pages used as sources, making the printed image of the type heavier than its form as originally cut or cast. This heaviness would have inescapably made its way into Morris's designs, even allowing for compensation. However, it was in any case undoubtedly the effect he wanted.

Morris's approach to book design inspired many initial imitators, trying to emulate his style as closely as possible, but it was essentially a backward-looking exercise that was too labour-intensive, and certainly too expensive, to take hold of a wider market – although the publisher J.M. Dent, with the

Everyman's Library of small, affordable editions of the classics, featured some beautiful Kelmscott-inspired title pages.

Golden has had its critics – Stanley Morison (*see* TIMES NEW ROMAN) considered it 'positively foul' – and its solid appearance, its overemphatic capitals, its role as an integral part of a graphic sensibility and philosophy, means that it can be equally adored or reviled. But it does have an evenness and clarity that can be admired and indeed loved. Beyond its own merits, it deserves inclusion in terms of importance because of its contribution to the visual output and philosophy of its creator. Morris was able to inspire without the need to adopt his aesthetic, and his approach to book design was invigorating. He looked beyond the single page to consider the double-page spread as a balanced, total entity, an approach that would find dynamic expression in photography-driven magazine design in the 1960s and later. Just one example of his attention to detail is shown in a spread for the Kelmscott Press's *The Works of Geoffrey Chaucer* (1896), considered the finest flowering of Morris's book work. The letter A occurred constantly where he wished to use a decorated initial letter for the start of each character's description in the Prologue to *The Canterbury Tales*. Multiple designs were created to maintain visual variance and avoid a repetitive and ultimately deadening effect to the pages.

Although Morris had other health issues that led to his early death in 1896, a contributing factor must have been his phenomenal work ethic, rising early every day to cram in more hours of production. Golden is a part of this, of one man's dedication to both an aesthetic ideal and a belief that beautiful things, created with love and honesty, could and should enhance the lives of everyone, with the ultimate aim of raising the spirituality of society. 'To enjoy good houses and good books in self-respect and decent comfort, seems to me to be the pleasurable end towards which all societies of human beings ought now to struggle', he wrote towards the end of his life, looking from the warm and comfortable side of the windows of his house on the banks of the Thames in Hammersmith and seeing people passing by from nearby slums. Aware of his own good fortune, Morris never ceased to be troubled by the sight, and to attempt to change things for the better, for everyone.

DOVES TYPE

FIRST APPEARANCE   1901, GREAT BRITAIN
DESIGNERS   EMERY WALKER WITH THOMAS COBDEN-SANDERSON
AND SYDNEY COCKERELL, BRITISH

A typeface that drove its creator to destroy it, to prevent what he believed would be its inevitable misuse, doesn't automatically qualify for pantheon status on those grounds, unless it has intrinsic worth. The Doves type has the latter, as well as inciting just such a reckless and, in the circumstances, illegal destruction.

William Morris died in 1896 and the activities of the Kelmscott Press ceased in 1898, but his work in publishing and book design had had an inspirational effect that was spreading far beyond the shores of Britain (*see* GOLDEN TYPE). It also had a similar effect in his immediate neighbourhood on the banks of the River Thames at Hammersmith. Thomas Cobden-Sanderson (1840–1922), whose Doves Bindery had bound the Press's books, conceived the idea of starting his own private press, with an eye to exploiting the Kelmscott's list of sub-scribers, people with sufficient means to afford Morris's regret-tably expensive productions. Morris' friend and typographic and printing consultant Emery Walker was approached to form a partnership, although Cobden-Sanderson's wife Annie provided the capital to finance the enterprise.

In true private press spirit, Walker and Cobden-Sanderson decided to create their own typeface. The photographic en-largements used to create Morris's Golden type were revisited as source material. Walker's recorded comments suggest that the true feel of Nicolas Jenson's type had not in his opinion been captured at the first attempt, while Cobden-Sanderson wrote of his desire to create 'the type of today' as a step towards his concept of the 'Book Beautiful'. The drawing work for this new type was given to Percy Tiffin, a draughtsman at Walker's photo-engraving company Walker & Boutall. Tiffin worked for months on the designs for the characters, but surviving drawings show a somewhat rigid incarnation of the concept, lacking the fluidity of the finished face. Much credit for its final appearance must consequently be given to the punchcutter Edward Prince, for interpreting what Walker and Cobden-Sanderson wanted, rather than simply mechanically copying the forms he was given. The first appearance of the type was in the Doves Press's debut, Tacitus's *The Life of Agricola*, but its most celebrated appearance is in the Doves King James Bible of 1903–05. It recalls the Golden type, with its large x-height, and its full, round forms, but is a lighter, slimmer and far more sophisticated offering, on closer examination in essence a Venetian slab serif – the serif sub-classification defined as Venetian most notably featuring an inclined crossbar on the lowercase e. In his *Edward Philip Prince: Type Punchcutter* (1967), F.C. Avis notes the earlier judgement of the British Museum's Keeper of Printed Books, Alfred W. Pollard, that the Doves type 'for the first time brought out the full beauty of the Jenson letter', while pointing out that 'the position of the dot on the lowercase i is noteworthy' – as indeed it is, drifting high and to the right of the stem of the letter.

The books to which it contributed were equally striking. Although the Press was inspired by Morris's example, in design terms the Doves books went in completely the opposite direction, a stark, stripped-down vision of typographic purity. Occasionally featuring extravagant or calligraphic initials, the pages are dense blocks of text, most tellingly in the Bible, verse breaks marked only by the medieval character of the pilcrow ¶, which was used to denote a new line of thought in a body of text, before the convention of the spatial paragraph break developed. This aside, however, where Morris had looked to the past for his ideal 'black' page of heavy type and dense illustration, the Doves Press set a model for the simpler and visually lighter 'grey page' of the century just beginning, fusing Morris's medieval and Renaissance touchstones with a modernist future.

Before long Cobden-Sanderson had grown dissatisfied with Walker's contribution to the Press. He had envisaged the partnership as a close daily collaboration, but Walker saw his role as that of a consultant. He had another company to run, and couldn't devote all his time to the Press. As the Doves books followed a similar design approach, it could be argued that once the style was established Cobden-Sanderson could be left to run things. The press's compositor J.H. Mason attested to Walker supervising the presswork and ensuring that the highest production standards were maintained. Cobden-Sanderson's diaries reveal him to be an intense character, following his working and aesthetic ideals with a religious fervour. Indeed he began to elide the Doves type with a wider vision of its place in God's creation and the universe. Walker's standards in terms of excellence were no different to Cobden-Sanderson's, but his was a quietly diplomatic, authoritative personality, opposed to Cobden-Sanderson's more highly strung, passionate mode of operation.

The partnership was broken up, with eventual ill feeling on both sides and legal action instigated by Walker. After some

PARADISE LOST
THE AUTHOR
JOHN MILTON

OF MANS FIRST DISOBEDIENCE,
 AND THE FRUIT
 OF THAT FORBIDDEN TREE,
 WHOSE MORTAL TAST
 BROUGHT DEATH INTO THE
 WORLD, AND ALL OUR WOE,
With loss of Eden, till one greater Man
Restore us, and regain the blissful Seat,
Sing Heav'nly Muse, that on the secret top
Of Oreb, or of Sinai, didst inspire
That Shepherd, who first taught the chosen Seed,
In the Beginning how the Heav'ns and Earth
Rose out of Chaos: Or if Sion Hill
Delight thee more, and Siloa's Brook that flow'd
Fast by the Oracle of God; I thence
Invoke thy aid to my adventrous Song,
That with no middle flight intends to soar
Above th' Aonian Mount, while it pursues
Things unattempted yet in Prose or Rhime.
And chiefly Thou O Spirit, that dost prefer
Before all Temples th' upright heart and pure,

16

THE DOVES PRESS EDITION OF JOHN MILTON'S *PARADISE LOST*, 1902,
SET IN THE DOVES TYPE. THE TITLE AND ORNAMENTAL LETTERING WERE
BY EDWARD JOHNSTON.

initial success, public interest in the Doves books was dwindling – possibly as a result of their stylistic similarity – and the venture was looking increasingly unviable. The type was by this point probably one of the Doves Press's few assured assets, and it was agreed that Cobden-Sanderson would have use of it during his lifetime, after which, should he predecease him, it would revert to the younger Walker.

But the more he brooded on this, the less Cobden-Sanderson liked the prospect. The artist Charles Ricketts, when he closed his Vale Press in 1903, dumped his type into the Thames; it is likely this image had stayed in Cobden-Sanderson's mind. In 1913 he consigned the matrices and punches of the Doves type to the river from nearby Hammersmith Bridge. In 1916 he began dumping the type in earnest and in secret at night, always in fear of apprehension by the police. On one occasion a boat suddenly appeared from underneath the bridge, nearly collecting an unexpected cargo of lead. Cobden-Sanderson's actions were dangerous, and, regardless of any contract with Walker, illegal. However, he persisted until all the type in his possession was under water. In his diary he recorded how he stood on the bridge reflecting on what he had done: 'Then I lifted my thoughts to the wonder of the scene before me, full of an awful beauty, God's universe and man's – joint creators. How wonderful! And my Type, the Doves Type was part of it.'

A small amount of the type, from the first batch cast, survived on dry land, used for a two-line Christmas greeting from Walker to his wife at the turn of the century. The Doves type remained a design that only existed through the books which were printed with it. This was an existence that was in essence intangible; printed impression can be variable, according to paper and ink quality, the care and skill of the printer, and, in the case of metal type, the physical condition of the type. So Doves remained in some respects a ghost type, its reputation maintained by the quality of the books it graced, and also by the bizarre story behind its disappearance.

But that story was to have a surprising postscript, nearly a century later. Although a digital version of the Doves type had previously been attempted, designer Robert Green decided to create his own version, which was made commercially available in 2013. During the preceding years, in what proved a tortuous creative process, he found himself becoming understandably obsessed not only with the typeface but also with Cobden-Sanderson himself. Staring down into the waters of the river by Hammersmith Bridge, Green wondered why no-one had ever tried to recover any of the type. Searching at low tide in the exposed bed, he found three pieces, slightly corroded but recognizable, surviving their century of immersion. He hired a diver to investigate further, and 150 pieces were recovered, much to the global excitement of type enthusiasts.

ARNOLD BÖCKLIN

FIRST APPEARANCE   ABOUT 1903, GERMANY

DESIGNER   UNKNOWN

If you were to pick the typeface that most epitomizes the style
of art nouveau, whose curved, organic forms and lines dominated the world of European avant-garde graphics, architecture
and product design in the late nineteenth and early twentieth
centuries, it would probably be Arnold Böcklin. Böcklin the
man (1827–1901) was a Swiss artist, whose work fell under the
category of symbolism. Darkness, brooding skies, brooding
nymphs, combative and rapacious centaurs, stormy seas with
naiads and tritons – these formed the backbone of his subject
matter. Probably his most famous and successful work was
Isle of the Dead (1886), of which Alastair Mackintosh wrote, in
Symbolism and Art Nouveau (1975): 'there was a time when an
engraving of his *Isle of the Dead* was as *de rigueur* in a fashionable house as a [David] Hockney would be today.'

The typeface that bears his name is equally dark, a
blackletter of the Jugendstil, the German manifestation of
the art nouveau aesthetic. So sleekly is it drawn, and so much
does it seem like the essence of the style has been woven into
each letter, that it comes as a surprise to find that it was not
the work of a 1960s' graphic designer, yearning for *la belle
époque*, but was contemporaneous to and a product of the
period. Designed and produced by the Stuttgart-based foundry
Schriftgiesserei Otto Weisert in the early years of the twentieth
century, it was named in honour of the recently deceased
artist. Exactly who designed it seems to be unrecorded. Each

ÆBCDEFGHIJKL
MNOPQRSTUVW
123456·XYZ·7890
abcdefghijklm
nopqrſstuvwxyz
Stuttgart·Heilbronn

PETZENDORFER
SCHRIFTENATLAS
NEUE FOLGE

VERLAG
JUL·HOFFMANN
STUTTGART

A SPECIMEN OF ARNOLD BÖCKLIN, FIRST SEEN IN THE *SCHRIFTEN ATLAS* OF 1903–05.

character is composed of the sinuous, tendril-like curves that epitomized art nouveau. The leg of the H sweeps down from what would have been the upper left serif; the O and Q are bisected diagonally in their counters by gloriously superflu-ous, undulating crosspieces. The tour-de-force characters are arguably the capital M, its left upper serif curving down and weaving through the stems to unite with its opposite number, and the L, a simple right angle discarded and in its place a flourish, curving back on itself and levelling off to thicken then surge upwards like the sign-off to a signature.

How popular Arnold Böcklin was when the typeface first appeared is difficult to gauge, but whatever heights of recognition it reached must have been easily surpassed by its golden age, the decade covered approximately by the period 1966 to 1976. Despite the prevailing hunger for modernity and innovation, much of youth and popular culture was infused, by the latter part of the 1960s, and lasting into half of the next decade, with a nostalgia for Victoriana and Edwardiana, and for art nouveau, its original full surge of popularity being from the 1890s up to the outbreak of the First World War. The appeal of the latter is not hard to understand; its extravagant, sensual imagery, its air of fantasy and of the fantastic, clearly inhabited the same spiritual and visual territory as the flower-power era and its accompanying psychedelic artwork. It was essentially the same mindset updated. Many of the diaphanously clad female figures that inhabit the work of Czech art nouveau artist Alphonse Mucha, so popular as poster prints in the 1970s, are only a few stitches away from the *déshabillé* of Woodstock.

Credit for the typeface's revival must go in the first instance to Mick Chave, who left the British dry-transfer lettering company Letraset in the mid-1960s to become type director at photosetting company Face. He found Arnold Böcklin in Ludwig Petzendorfer's *Schriften Atlas: Neue Folge* (reissued in the 1980s as *Treasury of Authentic Art Nouveau Alphabets, Decorative Initials, Monograms, Frames and Ornaments*), originally published in parts in Stuttgart between 1903 and 1905, and he re-created it and other art nouveau faces, such as Edda and Desdemona, for the photosetting era. His former employer Letraset also issued its own version of Arnold Böcklin in 1969.

Along with derivatives, it became a highly popular typeface of the cultural left field, used obsessively on record and book covers, until the arrival of punk and its starker accompanying aesthetic in the mid- to late 1970s. Photosetting company Face even offered Arnold Bold, as if the need might arise to add even greater visual emphasis to a face that was already un-missable through its sheer weight and extravagance.

Arnold Böcklin became synonymous with a design style, and thereby also became a visual cliché. Yet it remains with us, at present happily prominent on the high streets of Britain in the house style of café chain Patisserie Valerie. In what can often be a typographically predictable and conformist world, it's doubly welcome.

CLOISTER BLACK

FIRST APPEARANCE   1904, UNITED STATES
DESIGNER   MORRIS FULLER BENTON OR JOSEPH W. PHINNEY,
AMERICAN

Morris Fuller Benton (1872–1948) was the chief type designer
for American Type Founders, a determinedly self-effacing
company man who is credited with hundreds of designs for the
company with which he stayed for his entire working life.

American Type Founders had been formed in 1892, an
amalgamation of twenty-three companies which were under
threat from recent technological innovations. One challenge
came from the Linotype and Monotype typesetting and
casting systems, which required matrices but cast their own
'hot' metal type from molten metal that could afterwards be
melted down and reused to make more type. Another challenge was the automatic punchcutting machine developed by
Benton's father Linn Boyd Benton, which meant that punches
could be made by mechanical means without recourse to
the manual skills and experience of an individual. Both of
these developments struck at the heart of the businesses of
companies making and selling type. Benton senior had had his
own type company, Benton, Waldo & Co., one of those which
repositioned itself under the ATF umbrella. As well as all the
furniture and fittings for a print shop, ATF also sold printing
presses and, of course, type.

Morris Benton, an only child, who had had his own print
shop in the family home, joined ATF in 1896 after graduat-
ing from Cornell University with a degree in mechanical

engineering. He stayed until his retirement in 1937. His involvement with type began with the task of standardizing the heterogeneous array of typefaces which ATF had gathered from its constituent companies, rationalizing and making a standard ATF product. From there he moved to designing type. He is credited with over 220. Some were ATF revivals of earlier faces such as Bodoni and Garamond. Some were developments in type families of faces initially designed by contemporaneous American designers. Some of the bolder weights of Bertram Grosvenor Goodhue's highly successful Cheltenham, and the Goudy family, beyond Old Style, are credited to Benton, including a co-credit on the eternally popular Goudy Handtooled. His sans serif faces Franklin Gothic and News Gothic pre-dated the British and German work on the form. He also designed Century Schoolbook – perhaps the one of which he was most proud – Hobo, Clearface and the definitive Art Deco face, Broadway (*see* BROADWAY).

Benton kept his head down in ATF. Not for him the self-promotion for which Frederic Goudy was renowned, and by some reviled (*see* GOUDY OLD STYLE). But Goudy was a freelance operator, whereas Benton had, until the company hit financial difficulties in the 1930s, a secure position at ATF. Design-wise, he was a safe pair of hands. Producing type designs in metal was a serious financial commitment for the company, and the creative process was reactive, the sales reps finding out what printers wanted, and then responding. Much of Benton's work has a solidity to it, but no great sense of energy, flair or excitement.

Cloister Black, or, to give it the name its equivalent bears in the age of the personal computer, Old English, occupies a similar status to Comic Sans in the typographic firmament, owing its popularity not to being a favourite selection of

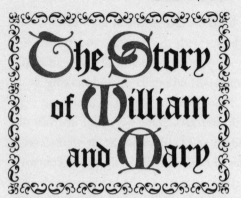

The Story of William and Mary

Written in Italian in the year 1422, translated into French by Raoul Georges a year later, and now done in English by John Watson and Mary Grover Sinclair

MCMXXIV

Publisher's Note

¶ This volume, although in no sense a facsimile of the style of the original work, is designed to embody the chief characteristics of the bookmaking of that period. Quarto in size, and printed on an imported hand-made paper in black letter, with rubrications as in original.

¶ Its illustrations comprise engravings redrawn from the woodcuts that appeared in the original edition and these effectually break up the uniformity of the rather solid pages of text matter.

¶ It is bound entirely uncut in covers of darkish green paper boards with a rough linen back and paper label. Three hundred copies will be printed, after which the plates are to be destroyed.

$15.00
a copy

Prosperity, Health and Happiness now and always · the Love of Friends and the fulfilment of your most cherished desires What more could I wish you on this your Birthday Anniversary? And I gladly do so

Richard Mitchell · The Hermitage · Worcester

MISSAL INITIALS   CLELAND BORDERS   CHAP-BOOK GUIDONS

383

CLOISTER BLACK, AS DISPLAYED IN AMERICAN TYPE FOUNDERS'
1923 SPECIMEN BOOK.

graphic designers, but by being a vernacular choice. Any establishment that prefaces its name with 'Ye Olde' will probably use it to represent that name. Similarly house name plates, particularly in rural areas, frequently use it. A personal favourite example was on the fascia of a South London tandoori restaurant, possibly because of a shared word in their names, Old Calcutta. It was an incongruous association of images, the English Middle Ages and Indian cuisine, but in terms of visual impact it undeniably worked. A probable reason for Cloister Black's popularity is that it looks important. Overcomplex though its capitals may be, unlike many black-letter faces they are at least legible (*see* FRAKTUR). So many people presented with a list of possible typefaces available for their house sign would home in on Old English because it has weight, it has blackness, the style is familiar, and looks impos-ing. A visual cliché perhaps, but imposing nonetheless.

It is a decidedly English blackletter; although, based on pen-formed letters, it lacks the jagged, tightly coiled aggres-sion of some of the German Fraktur-style faces and carries none of their negative associations. It brings to mind a world of benevolent English medieval figures – Dick Whittington perhaps, or Robin Hood. If the prince of thieves had fired a message wrapped around the shaft of an arrow through a slit window of Nottingham Castle, it would have been lettered in something very similar to Cloister Black, undoubtedly by Friar Tuck, a monk and therefore the scribe among the outlaws.

The style had the power of endurance, an essential player in any typefounder's list of stylistic offerings. William Caslon's 1734 specimen (*see* CASLON), to take just one example, features it under the generic name of 'Black'. If a printer wanted to emphasize words on the page in the eighteenth century, beyond increasing the type size it was the only option – bold versions of faces were yet to come.

Cloister Black was a 1904 offering from ATF. Credit for the design is sometimes given to Benton's colleague Joseph Phinney. One scenario is that Phinney came up with the idea, but Benton executed the designs. Certainly the face's American patent cited Benton as its inventor, and he later claimed it as one of his. In the immediately preceding years he had designed two other blackletters for ATF, Wedding Text, whose appearance suggested rather funereal nuptial celebrations, and Engravers Old English. Although not radically dissimilar, where Cloister Black possibly scored over the others was a slightly larger x-height, wider capitals, greater overall weight on the page, but a less-spiky, friendlier feel. Although there are differences in some of the capitals, Cloister Black follows closely the model of Caslon's Black, in its weight and proportions, particularly in the x-height to upper case ratio.

Why was ATF interested in reviving a basically archaic and impractical form? The fact that Benton designed three blackletters within about four years shows their popularity in the United States at that time. This was partly because blackletter had never truly gone away, having had a limited but dedicated typographic role in English text since the form had been abandoned for uniform usage during the Renaissance. In the 1890s William Morris and the Kelmscott Press had put the medieval back in the foreground in terms of typographic feel and book design (*see* GOLDEN TYPE). His style had been enthusiastically taken up by American presses, and arguably imitated more closely than by Morris's British contemporaries. So Cloister's design would have made sound commercial sense, a factor uppermost in ATF's mind since its foundation in 1892. Its decision has been justified over the decades. Ipswich-based printers W.S. Cowell, in their handsome 1952 type specimen, said of it: 'Cloister Black can be used effectively in jobbing work, particularly for an odd word or for a single line. A most effective quality can be achieved by the restrained use of this face in contemporary settings.' Its most current use, in the early twenty-first century, is in body art, ever popular as a lettering style for the skin. But if you're thinking of having a tattoo done, please don't use all capitals. They're a nightmare to read.

CENTAUR

FIRST APPEARANCE   1914, UNITED STATES
DESIGNER   BRUCE ROGERS, AMERICAN

> Having no reputation to maintain as a designer of types I
> have endeavoured only to produce a clear and legible letter
> that may be used in printing either ancient or modern works
> without attracting undue attention to itself.

Thus wrote Bruce Rogers in 1929 on the launch of Centaur
as a commercially available typeface for Monotype. This was
a typically restrained, modest public statement. But when
you possess a deep sense of your own personal worth, and are
happily aware that the regard of the world for your talents is
at least equal to your own, then self-deprecation only adds to
the esteem in which you are held. Although his name might
provoke little recognition outside of the graphic design profession, Bruce Rogers is considered one of the finest book designers of the first half of the twentieth century. Among American
fine press and fine printing designers and aficionados, arguably
no face is held in higher regard than Centaur, and no designer
higher than Rogers. Voice reservations about him in their
company at your peril – like a consignment of unilaterally
taxed eighteenth-century tea, you may find yourself unceremo-
niously dumped in the nearest harbour. Love of the typeface,
and love of the man himself, what he represented by his work,
go hand in hand. It's a configuration unparalleled in the world
of type. But both passions are justified.

Centaur is light, elegant, highly readable, and carries an air
of high pedigree, emanating from its source of inspiration, the

All seasons were alike to Pluto. Hell,
Not comfortless, nor only torment (far
From torment only since the impetuous day
When he had borne her down, Persephone,
From Enna's plains, his mistress and his queen)
Yet knew not change. In Hell no day and night,
Nor leaves to come and go, nor from the sun
Cool green of shades, lightened his caverned reign
Of easy gloom where, without any tides,
Voluptuous monotony was all.

THE FIRST, FOUNDRY VERSION OF CENTAUR WAS USED BY ITS DESIGNER
BRUCE ROGERS FOR JOHN DRINKWATER'S *PERSEPHONE*, PUBLISHED IN 1926.

Italian Renaissance. Without, as Rogers said, attracting attention to itself, it lends an unmistakeable air of style and refinement to the page. Nothing will look clumsy or heavy-handed with Rogers's thoroughbred setting the typographic tone. It was never a great success in terms of sales for Monotype; for more workaday setting and prose content it is perhaps a little too delicate. But the affection in which it is held persists, and Monotype still offers a digital version. It's unlikely ever to drop from the sales list. 'The design', say Jerry Kelly and Misha Beletsky in *The Noblest Roman: A History of the Centaur Types of Bruce Rogers*, 'possesses a degree of dignity and grace that is as sublime as it is impossible to replicate ... Centaur ... stands as a perennial classic, unaffected by time.'

Born in Indiana in 1870, Rogers, unlike many of his significant professional contemporaries of the early decades of the next century, did actually enjoy a formal college education in art. He worked first as an illustrator, an on-the-spot artist for *The Indianapolis News*, making drawings of fires and other disasters which would be converted into newspaper illustrations. He also had a spell working in a railway office.

Rogers's light-bulb moment came in 1893 when he encountered Joseph M. Bowles, an inspired salesman in an Indianapolis art store, who had started a magazine, *Modern Art*, which featured the work and aesthetics of the English Arts and Crafts movement, spearheaded by William Morris and his Kelmscott Press (*see* GOLDEN TYPE). Seeing its first issue and the Kelmscott books Bowles had imported for sale in the shop, Rogers decided that book design was where his future lay, and was given work on the magazine designing decorative initials and other embellishments.

Bowles moved *Modern Art* to Boston in 1895 to take advantage of the financial support of publisher Louis Prang, in an ultimately vain attempt to save the magazine. Rogers followed, and managed to secure employment at the Riverside Press in nearby Cambridge before Bowles's publication went under.

An overview of Rogers's design career gives the impression that not only did he never do anything he didn't want to do, but was extremely skilful in persuading others to see things his way, and to accept his time frames. He exudes the air of an urbane, unhurried graphic playboy, of another Bruce – Wayne. But Rogers had no need of an alter ego to perform his wonders. Even the U-boats of the Imperial German Navy seemed mindful of his gravitas, he and his family docking safely after a transatlantic passage to England in 1916.

He induced Riverside, a very commercially orientated company under the umbrella of publishers Houghton Mifflin, to devote part of its endeavours towards a fine press, Riverside Press Editions – smaller print runs, more expensive editions, designed by Rogers. During an era when the concept of the designer as a person and position quite distinct from the printer had yet to take root, he displayed his personal emblems at prominent sizes on the books' title pages. The earliest use of the term 'graphic design', in its modern sense, is attributed to fellow American designer William Dwiggins in 1922, but Rogers was making the distinction between the book's designer and its printer more than twenty years earlier, expressing a preference for the conceptual phase of the process alone.

Centaur was another product of Rogers's personal initiatives. He followed a similar line to Morris in his attempts to create a typeface, turning to Jenson and the early Italian Renaissance period for his models, a perceived superior, purer letterform to those currently in favour (*see* JENSON'S ROMAN TYPE).

In 1902, while at the Riverside Press, he had used his powers of persuasion to induce George Mifflin to let him create a bespoke typeface for the Press, to be used first on an edition of Montaigne's *Essays*, and taking as its inspiration Nicolas Jenson's 1470 type. Rogers hadn't been happy with the resulting face, Montaigne, feeling that the punchcutter had paid too little heed either to Jenson's original or to Rogers's drawings.

He may have begun a second stab at a Jenson-inspired type while still at Riverside, possibly as early as 1909. He enlarged pages from Jenson's edition of Eusebius' *De Evangelica Praeparatione* and, seeking to capture the calligraphic qualities he perceived to be in the original, drew his letters with a broad-nibbed pen, then retouched them. William Morris and Emery Walker with the Golden type and Walker with the Doves type had worked from enlargements of letters where spread of ink on the original paper had given them extra weight, a disproportion which had either to be imitated, in the case of Golden, or taken into account and compensated for, in the case of Doves (*see* GOLDEN and DOVES TYPE). Both have their appeal in their contributions to the books in which they appeared, but are very 'site-specific'. Used elsewhere they inextricably carry the flavour of the Kelmscott Press or the Doves with them. Rogers, working in a more instinctive and freer method, drawing upon his skills as an illustrator, produced something with far wider appeal. Its effect on the page is much lighter.

Centaur's serifs are far less weighty than those of the Doves, and overall there is greater contrast between thick and thin strokes. The subtlety of the curves in a character such as the capital D makes the corresponding letter in the Doves look like a slab serif – which, it might be argued, the face actually is. Like Doves, Centaur employs the Venetian style for the lower case e, with angled crossbar, and the sweeping leg of the capital R. The overall effect is of light and space, with an x-height that lends itself to approachability and readability.

Some accounts describe Centaur as being in effect a commission, capitals only, by Henry Watson Kent, secretary of New York's Metropolitan Museum of Art, for use by the Museum's press. Frederic Warde, in his article 'On the Work of Bruce Rogers' and subsequent book, *Bruce Rogers: Designer of Books* (both 1925), asserts that Rogers had already drawn the letters – Kent saw them, and wanted them for the Museum. Centaur's first appearance proper, in both upper and lower case, was in the 1915 edition of a translation of Maurice de Guérin's *The Centaur*, printed by Carl Purington Rollins's Montague Press, thereby giving the type its name. It was a 'foundry' type, a metal face produced solely for hand composition.

In 1928 Lanston Monotype approached Rogers to produce a version for them, as commercially available, machine-set type. Monotype Centaur was intentionally made lighter than the original, most apparent in the larger sizes, where the serifs became finer yet. But this modelling, coupled with its earlier subtleties, makes it a highly attractive headline face, in addition to its virtues as text.

Centaur was also distinctive in that its italic started life as an independent face. Arrighi was based on the type of Renaissance Italian scribe and printer Ludovico degli Arrighi, and had been brought into being in 1925 by Frederic Warde and Stanley Morison to print *The Tapestry*, a collection of poems by Poet Laureate Robert Bridges. Rogers professed himself unable – or perhaps unwilling – to design an italic, and suggested Arrighi as a companion, initially called Arrighi Italic and then, following commercial logic, Centaur Italic (*see* ARRIGHI).

GOUDY OLD STYLE

FIRST APPEARANCE   1915, UNITED STATES
DESIGNER   FREDERIC GOUDY, AMERICAN

Frederic Goudy (1865–1947) stands alongside Morris Benton (*see* CLOISTER BLACK, SOUVENIR, BROADWAY) as one of the most prolific type designers of all time. Although his total, in excess of 120, falls some way short of that of Benton, it must be acknowledged that Benton had the advantage of working within the design department of a large company, American Type Founders. Goudy was always the freelance operator, and his entry into the field was more tentative than Benton's, whose father had been a partner in a type foundry which was absorbed into ATF.

Goudy regretted, into later life, having had no college education; in addition to other short-term jobs he worked in real estate and as an accountant, returning to the latter profession for security after some initial small success with drawings of alphabets which he submitted to type companies. He experienced two fires, thirty years apart, which destroyed his premises and much of his equipment and archives. He started private presses. It was only after losing his position as a bookkeeper in 1898 that he finally decided, either through desperation or a sense of nothing to lose, to try his luck as a lettering artist, managing to secure commissions for cover designs from publishers. He even started his own short-lived magazine, *American Cat News*, for feline enthusiasts. He didn't consider his life as a professional type designer to have begun until 1911, when he was forty-six, and created Kennerley Old

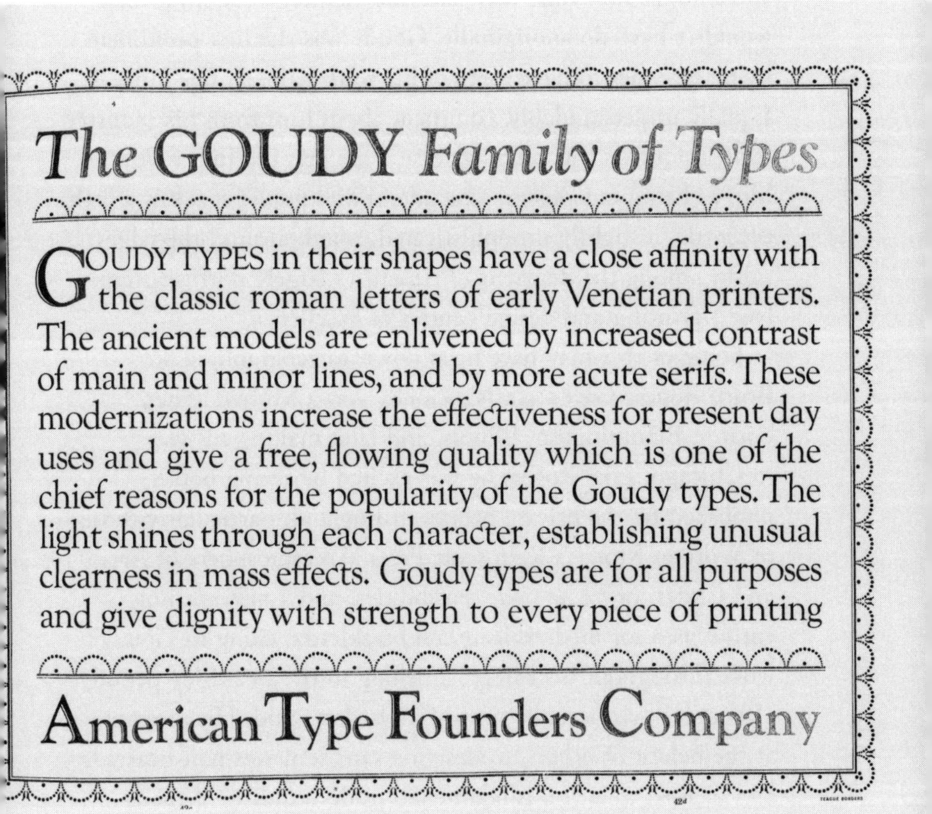

The GOUDY *Family of Types*

GOUDY TYPES in their shapes have a close affinity with the classic roman letters of early Venetian printers. The ancient models are enlivened by increased contrast of main and minor lines, and by more acute serifs. These modernizations increase the effectiveness for present day uses and give a free, flowing quality which is one of the chief reasons for the popularity of the Goudy types. The light shines through each character, establishing unusual clearness in mass effects. Goudy types are for all purposes and give dignity with strength to every piece of printing

American Type Founders Company

AMERICAN TYPE FOUNDERS HAD EXPANDED GOUDY'S INITIAL DESIGN, SEEN HERE IN THE MAIN TEXT, INTO A FULL FAMILY BY THE 1920S.

Style for the British-born, New York-based publisher Mitchell Kennerley.

Perhaps understandably Goudy was a relentless self-promoter, networker and enthusiastic attendee of celebrations given in his honour. He ran concurrent consultancy positions with type companies, unconcerned by any clash of commercial interests. Although revivals of types by Baskerville, Caslon and Bodoni now bore their creators' names, something they wouldn't have done originally, Goudy was the first prominent living designer to have some of his work named after himself. Equally understandably, comment about him from his industry contemporaries was often adverse. One gets the impression of him as being outspoken, a raconteur and public speaker, a little eccentric, a slightly unsophisticated, rough-around-the-edges misfit among the denizens of America's largely north-eastern-based printing and design centres of excellence.

Some of this may have been down to geography. Like Bruce Rogers (*see* CENTAUR), Goudy was a Midwesterner, born in Bloomington, Illinois, and later making his way to Chicago. Like Rogers he was excited by seeing books published by the private presses in England, particularly those of William Morris's Kelmscott Press. An atmosphere of Arts and Crafts, of *fin de siècle* sensibilities, and a never-failing enthusiasm for medievalism and blackletter, clung to Goudy's work throughout his career: 'I belong to the Beardsley period, although never actually part of it', he later said. His attempt, at the behest of others, to design a sans serif was half-hearted, and seemed to lack a fundamental understanding of the nature and self-imposed limitations of the form. Much of Goudy's output now appears to lack the crispness and strength of form that is evident in contemporary serifs, and whether most of it will ever return to vogue is questionable.

Even by the last decade of his life, the 1940s, American taste had moved to some degree away from Goudy, leaving him lamenting the influx and influence of European type and lack of support from domestic sources that had previously used his designs.

However, some of his creations have proved enduring, and one of these is Goudy Old Style. According to Goudy's own account, while on a visit to American Type Founders the company president Robert Nelson asked him to design something for ATF. Goudy agreed, on condition that the in-house drawing office was not involved. Although this was acceded to, the commitment was not honoured until Goudy complained. Goudy stated his source of inspiration to be 'a few letters of classic form from a portrait painting – I have always said "by Hans Holbein", but later search has never brought these particular pattern letters to light'. Goudy Old Style appeared in 1915, and was an immediate success. 'I am almost satisfied that the design is a good one,' he observed, 'marred only by the short descenders which I allowed the American Type Founders to inveigle me into giving p, q, g, j, and y – though only under protest.' He designed the italic but ATF, as was the company's objective with many of its faces, developed the Bold and Extra Bold weights to build a Goudy family, the development of which is credited to Morris Benton. Goudy voiced no stylistic complaint – except with Goudy Title, the Q of which 'irritates me mightily', he wrote – only a financial one. ATF didn't pay him for this development of his intellectual property, having bought his original drawings. It has been said that Goudy had fame, but never much money. After his death, his son Frederic Jnr was to reflect on the long hours worked, and time and money in shorter supply than that apparently available to other fathers in the neighbourhood.

As well as being an enduring text face, Goudy Old Style has proved popular in signage, particularly in franchise-owned pub and restaurant chains in the UK. The fluidity in some of Goudy's letterforms, which often translates into a sense of structural weakness, is here kept in check, making its presence felt to advantage. The vertical strokes have been described as looking as though they have been drawn with a brush, and the serifs have a similar quality – not quite straight, but straight enough, might be a good overall description of the face. It uses a classical structure, but looks friendly and approachable. The short descenders regretted by Goudy are an obvious advantage when used for display purposes; larger lettering can be fitted into narrower vertical spaces. Couple this with the face's generous x-height and it becomes very effective in terms of legibility in relation to available area. Goudy Handtooled, another ATF in-house studio production with a Benton co-credit, has, with its incised white inlines, been a similarly popular headline and signage choice.

LONDON UNDERGROUND

FIRST APPEARANCE   1916, GREAT BRITAIN
DESIGNER   EDWARD JOHNSTON, BRITISH

A typeface that starts life with, for its primary consideration, a
role in the environment, in the streets of a city, has a different
relationship with its audience than one designed primarily
for use on a page or screen. Its first responsibility is, as ever,
to communicate, but, beyond that, does it hold any further
obligations? The designer of what was originally known
as Underground Railway Block-letter, and now as London
Underground or Johnston Sans, Edward Johnston (1872–1944)
thought so, and saw his work as an aesthetic contribution to
the lives of all who passed within its radius – in a sense, art for
the people.

Johnston carried with him a sense of the deeply spiritual,
and his work was infused with it. In his Biographical Note to
Johnston's *Writing and Illuminating, and Lettering* (1906), his
former student Noel Rooke wrote: 'the importance of religion
in his life can hardly be overemphasised. ... For him all work
was a combination of prayer and praise.' It was a sense of the
near divine that he also communicated to others. Johnston's
most famous student, Eric Gill, experienced a 'thrill and
tremble of the heart' when he first saw Johnston working as a
calligrapher, and spoke of his 'subtle, painstaking, precise and
original mind' (*see* GILL SANS). It was as a calligrapher, who
had almost single-handedly inspired a revival in what had been
regarded as a moribund form, that Johnston's reputation was
built. Said Rooke: 'The intensity of his belief had such a hold

on him, and had such results in him, that it was possible to say, as Sir Francis Meynell did, "He was one of the few really great men of our time.""

Yet, for such an inspirational force, Johnston's early years were marked by a lack of direction, and his working years characterized by a determinedly unbusinesslike approach to the world of business, of diffidence and procrastination. He was notorious for letting commissioned work run very close to the deadline before starting, or sometimes not starting at all. Yet he seems to have been well served by serendipity. He had studied medicine at Edinburgh University but had abandoned the course through health concerns. In London in his mid-twenties, with a vague idea of pursuing a career in art, he was introduced to the architect Harry Cowlishaw, whose illuminated pen lettering in the magazine *The Artist* had impressed him. Cowlishaw befriended him, showed him how to cut a goose quill to make a broad-nibbed pen, and encouraged him to study manuscripts in the British Museum. Johnston, who had experimented with pen lettering when younger, now felt it was something he wanted seriously to pursue.

Cowlishaw was able to introduce Johnston to W.R. Lethaby, principal of the Central School of Arts and Crafts. Lethaby wanted to start an illuminating class at the Central School, and engaged Johnston as a teacher in 1899. Starting with seven students, the class size rapidly expanded once word spread. Johnston's approach was not that of the master instructor, but as the fellow explorer and seeker of enlightenment. Thomas Cobden-Sanderson of the Doves Press was one of his students, and Johnston contributed calligraphic embellishments to the austere beauty of several Doves publications, most famously a highly elongated initial I for the first page of the Doves Bible (*see* DOVES TYPE).

PRELIMINARY VERSIONS OF JOHNSTON'S UNDERGROUND RAILWAY BLOCK-LETTER, 1916.

The move from lettering with a quill pen to designing what was in essence a corporate bespoke typeface was not such a leap as it may seem. Johnston had lectured students on the need for better public signage. In what seems to have assumed the status of a golden evening in typographic legend, he was walking home from a class with Gill and Rooke, when the group were struck by the block lettering painted on a van's tarpaulin: simple, effective and sans serif. Here was a spirit to emulate. Johnston later gained experience in type design working with the German Count Harry Kessler's Weimar-based Cranach Press.

It is somewhat surprising that Johnston was persuaded to undertake the London Underground commission. He was opposed to the idea of mass production, or even to tackling a large project. Gerard Meynell, publisher of the short-lived but influential typographic journal *The Imprint*, for which Johnston created the title-piece, would feed him tasks in small doses to ensure they were done. It was Meynell who in 1913 introduced Johnston to Frank Pick, the commercial manager of the London Electric Railway Company, who was responsible for publicity and advertising, a remit which included signage. Meynell remained, at Johnston's insistence, his intermediary, a buffer for him against direct contact with an actual company and what it represented. Pick, a man of great taste and artistic vision, who was responsible for the commissioning of the many era-defining illustrated posters for which the Underground became justly celebrated in the interwar years, wanted a new typeface for the use of the Underground system. It had to speak of and for a modern age, leaving behind any trappings of the Victorian era, and be easy for the public to read, even from a moving carriage. It was Pick's idea that the typeface should be a block letter, that is to say a monoline, in which there would be no thin and thick strokes.

In true dilatory Johnston style, the next meeting with Pick did not happen for another two years, in October 1915, but following a third encounter the following month Johnston was promising him two or three alphabets by the middle of December. Eric Gill had accompanied Johnston to the second meeting, and did enough preliminary work on the face – dropping out because of the pressure of carving the Stations of the Cross for Westminster Cathedral – for Johnston to give him 10 per cent of the fee. Johnston only produced a sketch of a handful of letters by the target date, but at the start of 1916 his celebrated pressure-of-deadline focus came into play, and by February he had produced a first draft of the upper-case letters with alternatives. By July he had finalized both upper- and lower-case alphabets.

And so, seemingly painlessly, the greatest typographic contribution to the streets of London was born. It is possible that Johnston himself saw his design, perhaps with a typical disconnection from reality, as being for use on posters rather than signage. Ironically, on signage it looked wonderful, but on early posters, largely because of some atrocious letter and word spacing, it was somewhat less impressive. Although sans serif letters had been used previously for the fascias of Underground stations – and indeed a small number survive of these unsophisticated but vigorous letterforms – what Johnston did was to give a Roman classical proportion to the sans serif capital, imbuing it with grace, beauty, and a gentle authority. The lower case was subsequently less well regarded, Johnston resolutely applying a monoline even where curves meet stems, a place where normally they would narrow slightly to retain a consistent visual weight. But there is an unpretentious solidity and honesty to his lower case which enables it to retain its appeal, with some calligraphic quirks which have survived its

SOME ORIGINAL SIGNAGE STILL IN SERVICE OUTSIDE BETHNAL GREEN
STATION, LONDON.

1980s' updating; the diamond-shaped dots on the i and j, and
the 'hockey stick' l, conforming to Pick's dictum of clarity
and non-ambiguity of letter, have been retained. Some original
Johnston signage still survives.

One of the deepest reasons for the status of Johnston's
design is that, like the poster artwork that Pick commissioned, it represents the idea of art for the people. Whatever
their income, or the supposed lowliness of their professional
or social position, anyone walking the streets of the city, or
travelling through the Underground system, would have their
environment beautified, at no extra cost, by the work of some
of the finest graphic artists and designers of their era. No
mean offering.

SOUVENIR

FIRST APPEARANCE   1920, UNITED STATES
DESIGNER   MORRIS FULLER BENTON, AMERICAN

Souvenir was something of an oddity in the American Type
Founders stable, and its path to popularity was as a decided
slow-burner. Morris Fuller Benton drew it in 1914, taking as
a starting point a 1905 German face, Schelter Antiqua, which
carried in its genes a light influence of art nouveau. But he
seems to have been unconvinced by the result, or received
no encouragement to develop it; in ATF's monumental 1923
specimen book, Souvenir appeared in a range of sizes, from
6 point to 36 point but only as a single weight, and with
no italic. This was significant in a company that had made
a policy of development and promotion of the type family,
laying claims to have invented the concept. Type families made
sound business sense; convince an agency to buy one weight,
and you had a strong chance of selling them the others too, for
emphasis of the hierarchies of information in print advertising.
Benton himself didn't include Souvenir in the list he compiled
in 1936 of his designs.

Souvenir effectively dropped from view until 1967, when
it was revived for a client by Ed Rondthaler's New York-
based studio Photo-Lettering (later to amalgamate into the
International Typeface Corporation, ITC). Another, more
condensed version also appeared, drawn for Eastern Air Lines
and later commercially offered as Eastern Souvenir. In 1970
ITC offered ITC Souvenir in four weights with italics, created
by Ed Benguiat, and its success was now assured.

Recital of

Romantic Italian Music

Given by

MR. JOHN M. LIVERMORE

Under the auspices and direction of the Sophomore
Class of Bellwood University
November twenty-seventh at eight-thirty

Music Hall

This is the first of a series of six recitals to be given by Mr. Livermore during the winter

ANTIQUE ORNAMENT

EFFECTIVE
ADVERTISING
PRINTING

Is the necessary hand-
maiden of any
educational selling
propaganda or, in fact,
of every sales
campaign regardless
of its nature

ANTIQUE ORNAMENT AMERICAN BORDER

453

CONTRARY TO AMERICAN TYPE FOUNDERS' USUAL FAMILY-BUILDING POLICY,
SOUVENIR, SEEN HERE IN THEIR MONUMENTAL 1923 SPECIMEN BOOK, ONLY
APPEARED AS A SOLITARY ROMAN WEIGHT, PROBABLY DOOMING IT TO
FAILURE – UNTIL ITS REVIVAL IN THE LATE 1960S.

Souvenir sometimes makes an appearance in the 'worst ever fonts' lists so beloved of bloggers. The reasons for this are twofold: its ubiquity in the 1970s and 1980s, and its style. Interestingly, although ITC loved to create its own versions of classic faces by making them conform to the house style of big x-heights with short ascenders and descenders, Benton's original design needed no tampering on this score, taking its cue from the proportions of Schelter Antiqua. So Souvenir actually looked decades ahead of its time. Depending on one's aesthetic position, this proportioning alone can be enough to render Souvenir loathsome, but offence might also be taken by classicists at Souvenir's air of rotundity, its determination to avoid straight lines whenever it can. This was a characteristic taken from Schelter. Art nouveau was a style that experienced a resurgence in popularity in the 1960s and 1970s. Souvenir had found its time, and evokes strongly the era of ITC, and its house journal *U&lc* (*Upper & lower case*). It's a period piece, a workhorse that got worked too hard in its day, but in its favour it is highly readable. ITC's dominant stylistic light, the designer Herb Lubalin, was unenamoured of Swiss-style typography (*see* HELVETICA), believing its modernism to be too inexpressive for the American spirit, and Souvenir represents a graphic mood that stands far apart from it. Friendly and unsophisticated, it has been called 'a quintessentially American typeface' for these very qualities, ubiquitous in advertising and publishing as a display face.

Although totally anomalous with current tastes, in Souvenir's defence it has an appealing sense of lazy energy that much of Benton's output lacks, and sits very confidently and authoritatively in the space it occupies, ironically much in the way that Helvetica does. These two factors were surely the key to its great subsequent popularity and in managing, stylistically, to hit a note that would be right for the times it now lived in, half a century after its disregarded appearance in the 1923 specimen book.

Ironically the one souvenir Benton himself wanted following his retirement in 1937 was a copy of that book – it was his monument, yet he didn't have one. Of those still on the premises, no one was prepared to let him have a copy, he a loyal company man of forty years, on whose shoulders its typographic success and reputation had been built.

COOPER BLACK

FIRST APPEARANCE 1922, UNITED STATES
DESIGNER OSWALD COOPER, AMERICAN

Oswald 'Oz' Cooper (1879–1940) designed seven faces for the
Cooper family: the star, along with its italic and condensed
versions, 1922's heavyweight Cooper Black. Emblazoned on
every easyJet aircraft, it remains prominently with us in the
twenty-first century, but enjoyed prolonged popularity through
much of the twentieth – certainly up until the early 1980s.

Oz Cooper came from smalltown Kansas, 'the edge of the
Wild West' as he described it. Having interspersed his schooling with periods of summer holiday apprenticeships with a
printer, he moved to Chicago aged twenty with the ambition
of becoming an illustrator and enrolled in Frank Holme's
School of Illustration. Holme had built a successful career as
an on-the-spot artist and illustrator for Chicago's daily press,
and is remembered as an inspirational teacher; the School,
however, generated most of its income from correspondence
courses. As well as Cooper, it numbered among its students
the designer William Dwiggins, credited with coining in
the early 1920s the term 'graphic design'. On the teaching
side, as well as the fraternal giants of early-twentieth-century
American advertising and magazine illustration, J.C. and F.X.
Leyendecker, the type designer Frederic Goudy (*see* GOUDY
OLD STYLE) was to prove an influential instructor, not least to
Cooper. Before long he had abandoned illustration for lettering
and typography, so successfully that Holme gave him responsibility for handling that side of the correspondence work.

Holme died of tuberculosis aged only thirty-three, and the School gradually sank under his enforced absence through declining health, and growing financial problems. Cooper formed a partnership in 1904 with Fred Bertsch, handling all aspects of graphic work, including advertising and book and magazine design, and later typesetting. Lettering was Cooper's speciality. His first notable typographic success was through lettering he designed for the automobile company Packard; this was developed without Cooper's knowledge into a full typeface and marketed by American Type Founders in 1913. Later supplemented by a bold version, both are credited to ATF's Morris Fuller Benton (*see* CLOISTER BLACK, SOUVENIR, BROADWAY), or at least to its design department under his direction. To ATF's credit they did pay Cooper once the origin of the lettering was pointed out to them. Cooper's first face proper, Cooper Old Style, designed in 1918, was a loosely structured roman with rounded serifs, its letterforms revealing clearly the mark of the hand letterer, the dominance of the freehand pen unrestricted by the imposition of the ruler.

Cooper was a key figure in the commercial art industry of Chicago in the early- to mid-twentieth century. The city saw itself as a more down-to-earth, less pretentious counterpart to what Midwestern émigré Goudy called 'the effete East'. A self-effacing, gentle, quietly humorous personality, Cooper was cut from the same cloth, and seems to have earned the undivided respect and affection of his creative contemporaries. His authority came through his design abilities, coupled with sheer integrity. Under the terms of Holme's correspondence course contracts, the students had paid up-front for the full cost of the tuition, could halt the course at will and resume whenever they wished – the hope on the School's part being, no doubt, that they never would. With the closure of the School, Cooper

A TWENTIETH-CENTURY BLACKLETTER, STILL IN FLIGHT IN THE TWENTY-FIRST.

sorted out the finances as best he could, particularly for the benefit of Holme's widow, and personally honoured the unful-filled contracts. The extent of his even-handedness in this was illustrated by the story of the last of Holme's artistic revenants resurfacing seventeen years after the closure of the School – bizarrely, following the personal intercession of two nuns who arrived at the Bertsch & Cooper offices. Cooper honoured that contract too.

After an anecdote like that, it's hard not to like at least one member of Cooper's typographic output. Cooper Black's rounded serifs and the sense of structural looseness remained from its predecessor, Old Style, but its elephantine weight gave it a personality and presence on the page that Old Style had lacked.

Initially reviled by some American printers, on the probable grounds of profit-margin-nibbling ink consumption, and the greater care needed to maintain a solid uniform impression of the letters, Cooper Black immediately became a huge success, particularly among advertisers – its benefits when used for headlines were obvious. It was described as making 'big advertisements of little ones'. Its large x-height in relation to the ascenders and descenders made it particularly effective in filling available space, giving it an imposing presence on the page. It was a trait that would also help ensure its longevity, chiming stylistically with the later tastes and structural ethos of the International Typeface Corporation, whose designs and restylings of classic faces dominated American and British typography in the 1970s and 1980s.

It also represents, as did much of the output of ITC, a parallel stylistic stream to European modernism, which had begun in the 1920s, and of which Paul Renner's Futura (*see* FUTURA) was an example, and which flowered fully with Swiss design and typefaces in the 1950s and 1960s (*see* HELVETICA). Cooper's design work fits with the prevailing style in the United States of the period; free of conceptual design thinking or ideology, and broadly historicist, drawing on classic influences. Blackletter (*see* CLOISTER BLACK) remained very popular as a headline face, and American designers Morris Benton and Frederic Goudy both designed new faces in this style. Cooper Black can be seen as a twentieth-century blackletter; a gentle appropriation and reworking of the style's visual presence, updated for an American market, and channelling Cooper's more relaxed calligraphic style.

Cooper himself, quiet humour to the fore, famously called it the typeface 'for far-sighted printers with near-sighted customers', his later Black Condensed characters as 'No show-off, just plain folks like the Black'. Arguably it's that unassuming, Midwestern warmth that still resonates with Cooper

'For far-sighted printers with near-sighted customers'

Black. Is it a 'bad' typeface? Stylistically, from a hard-line modernist standpoint, it is perhaps indefensible, but its exuberance is hard to resist. It also has some great quirks, such as the backwards-leaning hook of the lower-case f, and the tail of the upper-case Q, making its character resemble an overburdened snail. Cooper Black works confidently on its own terms. It is instantly recognizable, highly legible, and emanates a sense of friendliness and good feeling – not inconsiderable factors. The calligrapher Paul Standard, writing in the 1949 tribute *The Book of Oz Cooper*, produced by Chicago's Society of Typographic Arts, described Cooper's letterforms as having 'a skeletal firmness and rightness. Their controlled masses and the allotment of white space about them – these are made to achieve his effects.' Like Oz himself, Cooper Black exercises that control lightly.

NEULAND

FIRST APPEARANCE 1923, GERMANY
DESIGNER RUDOLF KOCH, GERMAN

Neuland is a face that has received low-level criticism in the last few years, often appearing in online 'worst fonts of all time' lists. A lot of this ire is directed specifically at the later inline version, in which a line has been etched out of its heavy body. Largely because of its application, sometimes in a condensed form, and as an inline, in the graphic identities of the global cinematic and dramatic hits *Jurassic Park* and *The Lion King*, Neuland has been described as a 'theme park font' and condemned as lazy graphic shorthand for 'Africa'.

In fact Neuland is far more significant, and its origins and story much more interesting. Although the inline has its echoes in other work of Neuland's designer, Rudolf Koch, it dilutes and prettifies the sheer weight of the original face. Koch was born in Nuremberg in 1876; his family background was a creative one, his father a sculptor, whose early death terminated his son's schooling. Koch became a metalworker's apprentice, which also allowed him to attend drawing classes at art school. Deciding to follow the latter career path, he worked as a freelance designer, artist and illustrator until in 1906 he joined the Offenbach-based type foundry Rudhard, whose name would soon change to Klingspor. He remained with them until his death in 1934. He also founded a private press in 1911 with publisher and printer Rudolf Gerstung, called, with reference to their shared name, the Rudolfinische Press.

NEULAND AS FEATURED IN PRINTER W.S. COWELL'S 1952 *A BOOK OF TYPEFACES*.

NEULAND

TYPEFOUNDERS

ABCDEFGHIJKLMNOPQRSTUVWXYZABCDEFG 10
HIJKLMNOPQRSTUVWXYZABCDEFGHI 12
JKLMNOPQRSTUVWXYZABCDE 14
FGHIJKLMNOPQRSTUVWX 18 No. 1
YZABCDEFGHIJKLMNOP 18 No. 2
QRSTUVWXY 30
ZABCDEFGH 42
IJKLMN 54

WOODCUT DESIGN BY RUDOLF KOCH

NEULAND is a black-letter titling, designed by the late Rudolf Koch in 1923. It was used in this country for the Nonesuch Press edition of *Genesis*, with engravings by Paul Nash. The illustration shown here is from a block-book by Koch, entitled *Elia*, produced in 1921.

A year after the outbreak of the First World War, despite having a family and being thirty-nine years old, Koch joined the army in Berlin. From there he was sent to Serbia, then France and Russia, as he described it 'always with the fighting troops, and always as a private soldier'. Suffering from a weak heart and anaemia, he spent a period of his service in hospital, returning to his duties only to narrowly escape death from a grenade. His diaries detailed days of long marching, battle, fatigue and hunger. He was eventually discharged on medical grounds in the autumn of 1917. Despite Germany's defeat and the hard economic conditions of the post-war years, his deep faith in God remained intact. 'What I gained in experience by this period of my life is not to be expressed in words, but a careful observer of my work will notice the change that this period brought about in me', he wrote, a man described by a friend as having been 'a precision worker with the magnifying glass, a calligrapher bent over his parchment like a monk'.

It is probably impossible to analyse accurately the effects of someone's wartime experiences. Despite what they write or say about it, much may well remain buried, even to themselves. But Koch now entered the most productive period of his working life, and the output was equally striking. Perhaps this energy came through gratitude at having been given the opportunity to continue working when the odds had been against him, or an awareness, through his periods of hospitalization, that the time given to him might not be of great length. It was a heart attack that would eventually take him. He was to produce work of great power, but also of great delicacy, from his botanical drawings for *Das Kleine Blumenbuch* (*The Little Book of Flowers*) to his range of type designs: from the jazz-age favourite Koch Antiqua, also known as Locarno or, in its American incarnation, Eve, to the pioneering sans serif Kabel, the op-art forerunner Prisma, and in 1923 Neuland. 'All his founts', wrote Julius Rodenberg for the contemporary type journal *The Fleuron*, 'are derived from written hands. They spring into life quite freely...' Koch was to take this spontaneity a step further in creating Neuland.

Traditionally, to make metal type, the image of the letter had to be sculpted, as a reverse image, in a hard metal, usually steel. This was the punch, which was then struck into a softer metal such as brass, to make the matrix. This was in essence a mould with a positive image of the letter. The matrix was filled with molten lead, which would form, when it hardened, the piece of type; again a reverse image, which when inked and pressed to the paper would give the positive printed image. Usually drawings would be made first of the letterforms, which the punchcutter would use for guidance when cutting the letter. One of the things that is remarkable about Neuland, apart from its controlled informality, its weight and its sense of visual rhythm, is the fact that Koch cut the images of the letters directly onto the punches without recourse to drawings.

Examination of the different sizes of the metal Neuland reveals that corresponding characters at different sizes are not simply smaller or larger versions of the same form. They are subtly different; they retain the essential DNA of the design, are unmistakably Neuland, yet each is also unique, like a hand drawing from memory. It is a remarkable feat. The American designer Frederic Warde (*see* ARRIGHI) described Koch in 1929 as 'one of the really great geniuses of the modern time in book making', and Neuland is a testament to that genius. It works best en masse, where its monolithic power becomes fully apparent. Then it achieves real beauty, and captures the energy and movement of Koch's woodcut images, the violence even. But not everyone liked it, even at the time. According to Koch's colleague and collaborator Fritz Kredel, the foundry owner Karl Klingspor 'was less than enthusiastic. He called the design, in fact, "abominable, horrible, unbearably ugly," then added, "but go ahead, by all means. I am sure it will be a great success".'

Reading of Koch and his work, and that of his contemporaries in Germany, is a poignant experience. One realizes how quickly the country recovered culturally after the war, despite financial and political instability, and in just a few years became, stylistically and in terms of design philosophy, the leader of western and central Europe; how radical, idealistic and exciting so much of the work was, from film to painting to design, as typified by the Bauhaus school of art and design. Even more quickly, with the rise of the Nazis to power, that spirit would be dashed away, many of its proponents suppressed or forced to flee. Koch recorded his memories of his war service with the intention that 'for my descendants it holds, I hope, a number of remarkable memories, because I wish with all my heart that they will be spared the experience of living through such bitter and difficult times.' It was a vain wish. His son Paul, who followed his father into the field of type design, was lost, presumed dead, on the Russian front in 1943.

ARRIGHI

FIRST APPEARANCE 1925, GREAT BRITAIN
DESIGNERS FREDERIC WARDE, AMERICAN;
STANLEY MORISON, BRITISH

The story of the twentieth-century typeface Arrighi begins with
the visit of Stanley Morison, Monotype's typographical advisor,
to the United States in 1924 (*see* TIMES NEW ROMAN). It was his
first visit and, his reputation preceding him, the reception and
itinerary were too much for him. Overwrought, Morison spent
a certain amount of his stay avoiding people he didn't wish
to meet, and arguing with some he did. An oasis of calm and
hospitality was provided by the home of the American Type
Founders' assistant librarian Beatrice Warde and her husband
Frederic (at that point styling himself Frederique), who directed
the printed output of Princeton University Press. So well did the
trio get on that Morison managed to persuade them to abandon
their respective positions and head for Britain, to what was, in
terms of employment, an uncertain future.

Morison's original plan was to get the Wardes to help him
with *The Fleuron*, the typographical journal which he had up
to this point co-edited but which was now placed entirely in
his hands. Writing for the journal under a pseudonym to avoid
being dismissed out of hand in the male-dominated world of
typography and printing, Beatrice would begin to build her
career and reputation (*see* GARAMOND). Warde and Morison set
out to produce their own custom typeface.

Ludovico degli Arrighi, known as Vicentino, was born
around the 1480s near Vicenza. He worked as a papal scribe

and publisher, using type designs based on his own chancery script. He published fine limited editions of the work of fashionable poets, including the *Coryciana* of Blosius Palladius, Pope Clement VII's secretary of Latin letters. A copy of this, published in 1524, was in Morison's possession in early 1925. A page had been reproduced in an article he and type historian A.F. Johnson had contributed to the third issue of *The Fleuron*, 'The Chancery Types of Italy and France', and he had already featured Arrighi in his article 'Towards an Ideal Type' in *The Fleuron* no. 2.

Morison had also made the acquaintance of the Poet Laureate, Robert Bridges, who had himself a keen interest in typography, and had worked with Edward Johnston (*see* LONDON UNDERGROUND) in the years before the First World War on an abandoned project for a phonetic alphabet. Morison persuaded Bridges to supply him and Warde with some of his poems, which they would publish in a privately printed limited edition, using a new typeface based on Arrighi's type.

Morison and Warde saw themselves as being in a publishing race. Oxford University Press was shortly to bring out its own edition of Bridges's poetry, which they were felt would largely steal their thunder if it appeared first. Much of the body of the work on the face seems from surviving evidence to have been carried out by the Parisian punchcutters G. & H. Plumet, who were given the copy of the *Coryciana* that Morison owned, and directed to base what they produced on what they saw there. Warde then transmitted corrections and criticisms in response to their efforts. Bridges threw a spanner into the schedule by his sudden insistence on having two versions of the lower case g, to represent the 'soft' and 'hard' sounds of the letter.

The book, *The Tapestry*, appeared around the same time as the Oxford edition in late 1925, and was the first showing

Henricis," born at Vicenza, whence the appellation "Vicentinus." He seems to have taught writing first in Venice and then to have passed to Rome, where he finally occupied a position in the college of writers of apostolic Briefs in the Roman Curia. Unfortunately, search in the Vatican archives has not revealed any examples of his work as a scribe, and no details are known as to the date upon which he entered this post. The specimens of the chancery hand which he was the first to put out in book form in "La Operina da Imparare di scriuere littera Cancellarescha," (1522), were undoubtedly made while he was in the enjoyment of his official position—the title-page describes him as "scrittore de brevi apostolici." I have not yet succeeded in turning up any pieces of Arrighi's script, but he was surely a highly accomplished scrivener since "La Operina" is so well executed. It is a handsome work entirely devoted to the chancery cursive. Unlike many of the manuals which succeeded it, Arrighi's forms are very free and his hand untroubled with rules and compasses. The construction of epigraphic capitals on the basis of the square and circle as invented by Leonardo da Vinci and Fra Luca Pacioli yielded fine results; but to make, as Ferdinando Ruano did, cursive chancery upon the geometrical method means a much less satisfactory achievement

[x]

ARRIGHI, USED HERE FOR STANLEY MORISON'S INTRODUCTION TO FREDERIC WARDE'S 1926 EDITION OF *THE CALLIGRAPHIC MODELS OF LUDOVICO DEGLI ARRIGHI, SURNAMED VICENTINO.*

of what would be known as the foundry version of Arrighi. Cast in metal in just one size, 16 point, Arrighi was an attractive script, ornamental and flamboyant, while remaining highly legible. This was due to the flamboyance being largely contained in the ascenders and descenders, the latter sweeping, the former ending in curving, pear-shaped finials. The upper case letters were, in accordance with the style of Arrighi's day, uninclined.

The type now seems to fall under Warde's presumed and practical ownership. It represented a financial investment on which he hoped to capitalize, and he had second thoughts about the ascenders, which arguably made Arrighi just a little too distinctive. A second version of the type, called Vicenza, featured revised ascenders, now straighter and terminating in a sloping serif. Warde planned to design, or have designed, an Arrighi Roman, which this modified italic was intended to accompany, but the roman never saw the light of day.

Warde produced two further books in which he used Arrighi and Vicenza. But despite interest in and admiration for the type being expressed, hoped-for sales of Arrighi never materialized, possibly coming down to a question of price. Warde, his marriage to Beatrice having in the meantime come apart, returned to the United States towards the end of 1927. But early in the following year the question of Arrighi arose once more. The British Monotype wanted to market its own version of Bruce Rogers' Centaur – at that point, like Arrighi, purely a foundry type (*see* CENTAUR). Rogers, returning for a second professional sojourn in Britain, would supervise the conversion of his face. But he declared an inability or – probably with other, more seductive projects in mind – an unwillingness to design an accompanying italic, and suggested Arrighi as Centaur's running mate. In fairness he had already teamed the two faces, using them for an edition of the poet John Drinkwater's *Persephone* two years earlier.

This decision involved a complete redrawing of Arrighi, not just to fit Monotype's measurement systems, but also to make it balance with Centaur and that face's own parallel changes. Even with *Persephone* Rogers, limited to the one size of Arrighi, had to have it enlarged through photography and to print from metal plates made from the setting, to make it balance visually with Centaur. What Monotype would now rechristen Arrighi Italic had a larger x-height with consequently shorter ascenders and descenders, less inclined serifs as terminals to the ascenders, and an inclined upper case. In the company's 1929 prospectus for the release of the two faces, Arrighi Italic was described as a 'discreetly calligraphic design, in which all eccentricities have been abandoned in order to provide a graceful counterpoint to Centaur'. It was an accurate assessment; the distinctive earless lowercase g remained, but most of Arrighi's original individuality and panache was gone. In time the name was gone too; for sound marketing purposes it was called simply Centaur Italic.

However, the original Arrighi has kept a place in the hearts of designers, private presses and printing amateurs and enthusiasts, making intermittent appearances in print. Bruce Rogers described it as 'one of the finest and most legible cursive letters ever produced'. It is that legibility, linked to such luxuriant originality of form, that has kept Arrighi alive, carrying with it also an ambience of a period, the 1920s, when for many dedicated individuals the look and feel of a book, the type it was printed in, the binding, were all vital elements in the reading experience. Morison and Warde were two such believers. A version of Arrighi is available in digital form – a sloping upper case, but with pear-drop ascenders in place – as LTC Metropolitan, produced by the American foundry P22.

FUTURA

FIRST APPEARANCE   1925, GERMANY
DESIGNER   PAUL RENNER, GERMAN

Paul Renner's Futura has proved, along with Gill Sans, to be an enduring classic sans serif face that pre-dates the Second World War, yet still emanates a grace and style untarnished by time.

Despite crippling financial and political instability, in cultural terms, Germany made a startlingly swift self-reinvention after the First World War, moving almost immediately to the forefront of the European avant-garde. To take two celebrated examples from German cinema, *The Cabinet of Doctor Caligari* (1920) used low-budget but imaginative set design to create a nightmare world of insanity and abduction and the medium's first twist ending; Fritz Lang's *Metropolis* (1927) offered a stunning vision of a futuristic city and a starkly divided society that was both technically and imaginatively leaps ahead of anything that was coming out of Hollywood. Also in the year immediately following the end of the First World War the radical design school the Bauhaus emerged, whose influence and ideas still resonate through contemporary life.

It is easy to imagine the aircraft that ply the space between Metropolis's skyscrapers flying past advertisements set in Futura. The typeface is aptly named, as it strikes that so-difficult balance of looking both of its time and starkly up to date, achieving this largely through simple geometric shapes. Interestingly, Paul Renner (1878–1956) wasn't a type designer at the point that he began work on the designs for

REN
NER
FUTURA

DIE ERGÄNZUNGS-GARNITUREN

DREIVIERTELFETT

SCHRÄG / MAGER UND HALBFETT

SCHMALFETT

BLACK

BAUERSCHE GIESSEREI
FRANKFURT A · M · NEW YORK

FUTURA'S TIMELESS AND SEEMINGLY EFFORTLESS BEAUTY AND SIMPLICITY,
SHOWN ON THE COVER OF A BAUER SPECIMEN, 1930.

what would become Futura. He had begun his working life as an illustrator and painter, later moving into book design. In 1911, with designer and illustrator Emil Preetorius, he founded the Munich School for Illustration and Book Production, and continued to work in those areas, interrupted by war service as an artillery trainer. By 1924, having got through the period of runaway inflation in the young, unstable German republic by working for the Deutsche Verlagsanstalt, the German Publishing Association, he had decided to concentrate once more on painting.

But in the same year he met the publisher and printer Jakob Hegner, who was looking for someone to design a new typeface. The style of German book texts at this period was still heavily dominated by blackletter (*see* FRAKTUR) but debate over its retention or abandonment had raged since the nineteenth century. In contrast to this, new sans serif designs emerged from Germany in the 1920s, notably Jakob Erbar's eponymous design, Herbert Bayer's Universal type, and Rudolf Koch's Kabel. Hegner was excited to learn that Renner was a painter as well as a designer; he believed that the design of the kind of type he was looking for could best be achieved by someone who wasn't actually a type designer. He had already commissioned a typeface from the painter and Bauhaus professor Lyonel Feininger. 'The typeface of our time' was how Renner later recalled Hegner's description of what he wanted. However, after initial enthusiasm for Renner's first efforts, Hegner was unresponsive. Renner showed the drawings to Heinrich Jost, a consultant at the Frankfurt-based foundry Bauer. When the foundry's director Georg Hartmann saw them he was impressed enough to engage Renner to continue with his development, and then to put the typeface into production.

Renner certainly embodied Hegner's idea of an unprejudiced mind on the subject, as Renner later could not recall ever having used a sans serif in his book designs, and his own 1922 publication *Typografie als Kunst* (*Typography as Art*) was set in blackletter. Renner subsequently claimed naivety in failing to grasp how long a typeface would take him to design, revealing his ideas in progress through a trial cut of the face in 1925, allowing others to take inspiration from his ideas and produce parallel designs in the field that pre-empted him in commercial availability. He was defensive of his inspirations, claiming to have no knowledge of Edward Johnston's work for London Underground, or for similar typographic lines of thought being explored at the Bauhaus (*see* LONDON UNDERGROUND).

Renner had previously regarded sans serif as a somewhat debased form, but injected the proportions and form of classical Roman inscriptional capitals. 'I did not want to glorify the compass as a tool, instead I wanted to lead form out of the wilderness and back to its origins', he later said. However, he also didn't want the lower case letters to carry any trace of handwritten forms, and regarded them as the innovative part of his overall design. The lower extremity of t and j ended as a straight line, not a curve, and there was an alternative version of the r – the connected vertical stroke and curving finial replaced by an unconnected 'ball and stick' – and a square-cornered m and n. Although these, plus alternative forms of the a and g, were featured in several proof stages, and some appeared in the first specimen on Futura's release in 1927, to Renner's regret they had been dropped by the second specimen in 1928. He remained attached to some, and subsequently used them in his designs, seeing them as an attempt to reach pure forms with the lower case. But without them Futura as an overall design became consistent, and undoubtedly more commercially successful as a result.

Although Futura can give the initial impression of being formed purely by geometry, of course – as Edward Johnston discovered – a monolined circle cannot just be joined to a monoline stroke to form b or p. The line thickness must be modulated where the elements join, and it is this care in construction that gives Futura a sense of grace that could not be produced solely with a ruler and a compass. Contrary to its creator's opinion, its true power and beauty, unlike many typefaces, lies in the upper case. Renner's appreciation of form, weight and proportion, a grace that is immediately apparent, give them a power that is worn lightly. The M, V and W, with their width, inclined strokes and pointed junctions, hold a particular beauty.

Futura was released with Hegner's line 'The typeface of our time', and such was its growing success that the second specimen could announce: 'Futura, which conquers the world'. In the 1930s its royalties helped Renner to survive when those with ideas of a different form of world domination removed him from his teaching position and restricted his ability to work, and its popularity remained undiminished at the end of the war. The Nazis, while it suited them, enforced blackletter as the only true German typeface. Renner was judged 'untrustworthy' and, with his type, his opinions and his associates judged antipathetic to the new regime, narrowly escaped imprisonment. As late as 1944, with the implication of some of his relations in the failed assassination attempt on Hitler, Renner and his family came close to arrest by the Gestapo. Art, graphics and typography in Nazi Germany could be potentially life-threatening pursuits.

BROADWAY

FIRST APPEARANCE 1928, UNITED STATES

DESIGNER MORRIS FULLER BENTON, AMERICAN

The 1920s' tag 'the jazz age' conjures up images of young men in white tie and tails and young women with short hair and long strings of beads frantically dancing the Charleston to the sound of popping champagne corks. It is an image that, of course, overlooks the poverty and political crises of the period, but for a lucky few there were major sea changes in style and thought in this period, and an increasing gulf between those old enough to have fought in the Great War and those too young to have served, enjoying their youth in an albeit brief period of peace. Creatively it was an intensely fertile period, in terms of literature, painting and graphics, while bearing, for subsequent generations, the added frisson of being sandwiched between two world cataclysms, the decade flavoured at one end by the shell-shocked aftermath of the slaughter of the Great War, and at the other by the inexorable rise of fascism that led to a new and even more devastating conflict.

The typeface that encapsulates the 1920s and 1930s is Morris Fuller Benton's Broadway. For the company that produced it, American Type Founders, it represented at least one successful attempt to reflect a visual aesthetic that was, spiritually, moving beyond the tastes of the company's now ageing leading lights.

Broadway is sans serif, with extreme contrast between the thick and thin strokes, angular and geometric in approved deco style, a 1920s fat face. It is highly legible, with no weak

BROADWAY

A B C D
E F G H
I J K L
M N O P
Q R S S
SS T U V
W X Y Z
& $ 1 2
3 4 5 6
7 8 9 0
. , - ,
: ; ! ?

72 Point 3A

SHORE

60 Point 3A

KINDLE

48 Point 3A

GRANTED

42 Point 4A

DELUSIONS

36 Point 5A

NICE PERSON

30 Point 6A

ELECTROTYPER

24 Point 8A

MODEST REPORTER
INTERESTING LADY

18 Point 10A

STORM DAMAGES FLOWER
RARE SHRUBS DESTROYED

14 Point 13A

**UNCOVERED
HISTORICAL**

12 Point 14A

**INVESTIGATED
LITTLE HOMES**

10 Point 17A

**POPULAR YOUTH
SUPERIOR GUIDE**

8 Point 19A

**MOUNTAIN VACATION
ENJOYABLE HUNTING**

6 Point 20A

**INTERESTING EXPEDITIONS
NATIVE BOUGHT COSTUMES**

100

SPECIMEN OF BROADWAY, SHOWN IN AMERICAN TYPE FOUNDERS' 1941 *BOOK OF AMERICAN TYPES.*

characters, and has a sense of great solidity and balance, no doubt a key to its success, both initially and into the following decades, as subsequent generations fell for the fashion, art and graphics of the era. Broadway was originally caps only; a condensed version released in 1929 included a lower case.

Until the economic crash of 1929, the decade was one of boom for many in the United States. Printing industry trade journals of the period, such as *The American Printer*, exude an air of bubbling confidence that, through hard work and close attention to your business and to the needs and desires of your customers, the rewards are there, ready for the taking.

For American Type Founders, the 1920s were good times too. 1926, during which Benton was working on the design of Broadway, was its most profitable year. But the company's management were men of the 1890s, and the pace of change and the watershed of a world war meant that the turn of the twentieth century now seemed an aeon away. Inspirational company president Robert Nelson died in that boom year of 1926, and financially this was as good as it was going to get for ATF. From now on they would have a battle on their hands.

Typographically, there were new kids on the block. In 1925 Melbert Cary, formerly of the Remington Typewriter Company, set up Continental Typefounders Association in New York, bringing into the United States new European designs and casting them to conform to American specifications of size. A bitter turf war broke out towards the end of the decade. The German foundry Klingspor produced Rudolf Koch's Koch Antiqua, later renamed Locarno, and marketed by Continental in America as Eve. Despite bearing a strong calligraphic influence, Eve became itself something of a period classic with its condensed, upright lower case, made distinctive by the small x-height and attenuated ascenders. In 1929 ATF

THE QUINTESSENTIAL TYPEFACE
FOR SUGGESTING THE GLAMOUR
OF HOLLYWOOD AND OF THE LATE
1920S AND 1930S.

launched Rivoli. Rudolf Koch called ATF a 'highway robber
of German intellectual property', while the Americans in their
response freely admitted that the similarity between Rivoli
and Koch Antiqua/Eve, far from being accidental, was quite
deliberate, Rivoli having been created both as a spoiler for the

popular Eve and as a 'reprisal' face for what it claimed were numerous pirated American faces among those offered for sale by Klingspor's owner, Stempel.

In the second half of the 1920s ATF had been trying to respond to contemporary trends in advertising by producing some faces to reflect the spirit of the age. Much of ATF's design policy was reactive in spirit. Such was the cost of producing a new face in metal that caution had to be exercised: salesmen would ask printers what they would like or need, and report back. Head type designer Morris Fuller Benton, despite being born in 1872 and no jazz ager, designed a small number of advertising headline faces in the deco spirit in the late 1920s: Modernique, Chic, Louvaine, Parisian, Dynamic. When he produced a list in 1936 of what he considered his best or most significant designs, only Parisian featured from these, along with his most enduring creation in this style group, Broadway.

Broadway was inevitably included in the headline listings of photosetting companies of the 1970s and 1980s, and is offered in the twenty-first century by online dealers such as MyFonts, who rightly describe it as the 'quintessential Art Deco typeface'. Monotype produced its version of the original in 1929 with the addition of a lower case, designed by Sol Hess, a digital version of which is what is available today. Although it might be argued that Benton's customary solid, unflamboyant approach robs the face of much energy and of any unpredictability, Broadway has become a visual cliché, an inevitable by-product of its era-defining status.

GILL SANS

FIRST APPEARANCE   1927, GREAT BRITAIN
DESIGNER   ERIC GILL, BRITISH

Eric Gill was a giant in the British creative landscape in the years between the world wars: a sculptor, illustrator, wood engraver, letter-cutter, founder of private presses, writer and type designer. Like Stanley Morison, his Catholic faith under-pinned his life and his art. He formed working communities in which he was the central element, a master and teacher of like-minded disciples. Such was his personal aura that one visitor believed they could see a 'nimbus', a halo, around Gill's head. He was forthright and uncompromising in his opinions. Even his dress ran counter to the norm: wide-brimmed hats or the square, paper box-hats made and worn by carpenters; stonemasons' smocks and woollen leggings, with preferably no trousers. Made a Royal Designer for Industry, he was courted by the establishment while rejecting its values. His sculptures are on the exterior of the BBC's Broadcasting House.

Outspoken in his autobiography, both of himself and others, the part of his life in which Gill ran most counter to society's values was not touched upon, albeit faintly hinted at, until after his death. Fiona MacCarthy's 1989 biography *Eric Gill*, following a close reading of his diaries, revealed that her subject's Catholicism encompassed sexual relations with his daughters and his sister, on one occasion following attendance at a service at the Catholic cathedral in Westminster.

Gill (1882–1940) was the second child of a family of thirteen. Born in Brighton, he trained as an architect in

GILL § SANS
SERIF
☞ CAPITALS ONLY ☜
AT PRESENT

N ✳ B

IT IS HOPED
THAT A LOWER CASE
DESIGNED BY ERIC GILL
WILL BE PRODUCED
DURING THE YEAR
1928

London, but quickly grew to hate the profession, the lack of creative control afforded the workers who constructed the buildings and the irrelevance of their emotional involvement with what they were making. His attitudes chimed to a large extent with the ideals of William Morris (*see* GOLDEN TYPE). His boyhood enthusiasm for lettering led him to attend classes at London's Central School, where the teacher was Edward Johnston (*see* LONDON UNDERGROUND). Gill found Johnston inspirational, and worked with him on the initial stages of his Underground Railway Block-letter. An early prestigious commission was the carving of the low-relief Stations of the Cross for Westminster Cathedral. Gill's work was interrupted by a few months in army training camps in the final weeks of the First World War, his misery compounded by having to shave off his beard. But during the 1920s his reputation rose steadily. In 1926 his friend Douglas Cleverdon asked him to paint a fascia for his antiquarian bookshop in Bristol, for which Gill used a sans serif letter. It seems likely that Lanston Monotype's Stanley Morison, visiting the shop and seeing the lettering, conceived the idea of asking Gill to design a sans serif alphabet for Monotype, as a response to those emerging from Germany at this

PENGUIN
BOOKS

THE DARK
INVADER

ADVENTURE   ADVENTURE

CAPTAIN
VON RINTELEN

COMPLETE   UNABRIDGED

TWO WEIGHTS OF GILL AS USED IN THE CLASSIC 1930S' PENGUIN LIVERIES (ALTHOUGH THIS 1936 OFFERING APPEARS TO HAVE A ROGUE A IN THE TITLE SETTING).

period. When Morison had initially approached Gill to design a typeface, Gill's reaction had been to reply 'not my line of country'. But he had designed a serif, which became known as Perpetua. Some consider his most successful type design, and perhaps his best text face, to be Joanna, designed in 1930. Gill Sans was intended to be used as a text face, but, possibly too distinctive, it never really achieved popularity in that role.

Where it has built its longevity is in the kind of role it first played outside Cleverdon's shop: display and headline lettering, or used at most in small blocks of text. Unlike Futura, where Paul Renner tried to eliminate any sense of the hand-drawn letter, the strength and character of Gill Sans are particularly apparent in the lower case; you can feel that the letterforms are the work of the human hand. There is no rigidity; instead a subtle, organic grace. Gill Sans has come to represent two overlapping ideas: Britishness – an elusive quality to pin down in a typeface, but which unmistakably exists – and the time period encompassing the 1930s and 1940s.

In 2008 a viral graphic phenomenon appeared in the UK, the 'Keep Calm and Carry On' poster. This was the unissued third of a series of Second World War morale-stiffening posters, to be posted only in the event of an actual German invasion. Secondhand book dealer Barter Books in Alnwick, Northumberland, chanced upon a copy folded among some new acquisitions, and started producing facsimiles. Coinciding with the onset of the global financial crisis, there was something about the classic British understatement of the message that both amused and struck a note of topicality. The styling is simple: a red background, the text in centred, white hand-drawn capitals that spiritually walk hand in hand with Gill Sans, surmounted by a crown graphic. The original design spread like wildfire, and moved from posters to greetings cards, mugs, tea towels, fridge magnets and teddy bears, while spawning numerous spin-offs ('go crazy and freak out' as just one example) in various colours. When their producers have been faithful to the original styling, the lettering is Gill Sans. As well as the messages, the appeal and longevity of this theme are due in some part to the crisp simplicity of the graphics and the elegance of the typeface. Such is the beauty of Gill Sans that it can work, and perhaps does work, most effectively large, in white or a pale colour, on a plain background of a strong and distinctive colour.

And what of its creator? In the light of Gill's behaviour over so many years, it would have been thought inevitable that the whole thing would have exploded in his face during his lifetime – breakdown, revelations, accusations, estrangement. Yet none of this happened. Gill went to his relatively early grave with the status quo of his life intact. Even in the late 1920s, after years of knowingly living a very one-way open marriage, Gill's wife Mary wrote: 'I am simply bubbling all over with pride at the thought of being your wife.' We are left with images of comfortable domesticity, Mary with her tea-cosy-patting ritual each time she poured out the beverages. At his funeral, with northern European restraint, she transferred with her finger a kiss onto Gill's now cold lips. The malign power of his personality enabled him to do exactly what he wanted, while convincing everyone else involved that this was the proper order of things.

There have been calls voiced online for a boycott of use of his typefaces. Can we, should we, separate the artist from his work? Adrian Shaughnessy in *Graphic Design: A User's Manual*, asked, 'Is it possible … for something to be evil and also beautiful?', a question, perhaps unsurprisingly, he left hanging. But however repugnant we might find Gill the man, Gill Sans remains an enduring typographic great.

TIMES NEW ROMAN

FIRST APPEARANCE   1932, GREAT BRITAIN
DESIGNERS   STANLEY MORISON & VICTOR LARDENT, BRITISH

The name tells the story, to an extent. Times was originally designed, and is periodically redesigned, for *The Times* newspaper. It did not come about as a designer's whim, and although aesthetics did, and do, play a part in its design history, the primary considerations, and the reasons for its regenerations, were technical, responses to the changing technologies and physicalities of newspaper production. Released for universal sale a year after its first appearance in the newspaper's 3 October 1932 issue, it has remained a giant of the typographic firmament ever since, its popularity helped further by the rise of the personal computer in the 1990s. Times was the default font for Microsoft Word until Word 2007.

Times will always be associated with Stanley Morison. He was born in 1889 in Wanstead, on the edge of East London. His father, a sometimes violent heavy drinker, deserted his family, leaving Morison's mother Alice to bring up her three children, supporting them by working in a tobacconist's shop. She managed nevertheless to find time for the life of the mind, and was an adherent of the political theorist and activist Thomas Paine and a decided freethinker. This was the political atmosphere Morison grew up in, although, perhaps incongruously, in his late teens he joined the Catholic Church.

Those who worked in the graphic arts in the early decades of the twentieth century sometimes liked to pinpoint anecdotal moments of revelation that convinced them to change career path, or to take a certain aesthetic decision or direction. This was in part because so many had not taken the route open to most aspiring graphic designers today – leave school, take a university design course in the subject, then seek employment in the industry. Also they must, over the years, have been asked so often the question 'How did you get into this line of work?' that the stories became burnished in the retelling. Many of Morison's era started their working life in a different profession. He himself was a bank clerk, though not a very contented one. His 'blinding flash' came on 10 September 1912, and perhaps fittingly *The Times* was the catalyst. To celebrate its 40,000th edition, it produced a 'Printing Number' supplement, which included, intoxicatingly for Morison, articles on the history of printing. But there was also an advertisement for a forthcoming printing industry journal, *The Imprint.* Morison bought the first issue in January 1913, and saw their request for a young man 'of good education' and preferably printing and advertising experience. Morison had neither of the latter, but got the job anyway.

The life of *The Imprint* was not a long one, but it gave Morison a start, and connections. His progress was hampered only by a spell in prison as a conscientious objector during the First World War. In 1922 he became typographic adviser to the British, and more vibrant, arm of the American type company Lanston Monotype. He assumed a similar role for Cambridge University Press in 1925. Morison threw an ever-increasing knowledge and a formidable personality into the development of Monotype's series of type revivals that drew on historical sources, sometimes from types created during but unavailable since the Renaissance. He became a 'big figure' in the world of type, possibly the biggest of his age. In the aesthetic landscape of the stylistically debased typefaces that were in general use

Specimens of 'Monotype'
Times New Roman
and its related type faces

designed, tested and commissioned by

THE ✦ **TIMES**

to achieve new standards of legibility.

The Monotype Corporation Limited
had the honour of assisting *The Times*
throughout the period of experiment,
by cutting thousands of patterns, punches, etc.
The basic upper and lower case shown here, &
THE FIVE RELATED TITLING SERIES
together with related Bold Faces, Italics, etc., comprising no fewer than 70 founts,
were approved, and adopted by *The Times* in
1931. One year later, the Monotype Corporation
was permitted to place this entire repertory on
the market, and since that time the world-wide success of
this 'Monotype' face has led to the extension of the repertory by
the cutting of a Semi-Bold and a widened version for Bookwork.

AFTER TIMES'S FIRST YEAR OF LIFE BOTH MONOTYPE AND LINOTYPE WERE
ABLE TO OFFER THE FACE FOR SALE IN THEIR LISTS.

in Britain before the war, worsened by indifferent printing, Morison was a significant force in making type design a major consideration. Schooling himself in what he considered the beauties of the past, he attempted, successfully, to channel that spirit into the contemporary world.

In October 1929 *The Times* produced another 'Printing Number'. Legend tells that when the newspaper approached Monotype with a view to them placing an advertisement in the supplement, which *The Times* would helpfully typeset, Morison retorted that he would rather pay them £1,000 *not* to set the ad, so low was his opinion of their typographic standards. This outburst reached the ears of the paper's management. Morison was invited to make proposals to improve *The Times*'s typography, and was appointed typographic advisor in 1930. Shown two type design proposals the following year, the committee selected a 'modernised Plantin', which subsequently became Times. Morison worked with Victor Lardent, an in-house graphic artist for *The Times*, who normally drew lettering for advertisers who had no agency to handle such matters for them. The new typeface, when it debuted on 3 October 1932, was more economical in terms of space than its predecessor, one key factor. The paper informed its readers that 'everything freakish or precious has been diligently eschewed and design in the headings and the body of the paper has been healthily subordinated in the strict purpose of aiding the eye.'

Monotype called the face Times New Roman to distinguish it from the 1908 'Times Old Roman', while competitor Linotype, when it marketed the face through its typesetting systems, called it simply Times Roman.

The origins of Times, from subsequent accounts, are a little hazy. In one version, to which Morison seemed to subscribe, he handed Lardent pencilled drawings of the letters. His ability to create such drawings to any usable standard has been questioned, and Lardent later said he received no drawings, but rather a photograph of a page from a book by Renaissance printer and publisher Christopher Plantin. Although much writing about Morison in the years before and after his death in 1967 was the work of friends and colleagues, and consequently eulogistic, someone with the amount of power he wielded would always be subject to some later reassessment. Such lack of clarity in the story of Times's creation left room for exploitation, and in 1994 an assertion appeared in the American journal *Printing History* that Times was in fact a pirated design, taken from an earlier face designed by, or created for, American engineer and boat designer Starling Burgess, which was never paid for and had languished in the Monotype files, resurfacing briefly in the 1920s in a proposed masthead design for the planned *Time* magazine. On the evidence presented the assertion has the appearance of, if not a deliberate hoax, then at least a Swiss cheese in terms of the number of holes in the story. But the fact that such an attempt was made shows the pre-eminence of Times, the cultural ballast it carries, and also the dominance that Morison, a sometimes overbearing figure, exerted over the typographic world. And, of course, people love a conspiracy theory.

Times has been periodically reassessed and overhauled as Times Europa (1972, designed by Walter Tracy), Times Millennium (1991, designed by Aurobind Patel and Gunnlaugur Briem), Times Classic (2002, designed by Dave Farey and Richard Dawson), and the headline family of Times Modern (first appearance 2006, designed by Luke Prowse at Neville Brody's Research Studios; see ARCADIA). The changes have addressed such questions as body width and performance in terms of inked impression, as the newspaper's printing technology and its page size have changed through the decades. But the face remains indisputably Times, its essential DNA preserved. The initial anomalies between the weights, probably a result of the design work being farmed out in haste to other agencies, have been ironed out over time. Morison himself was restrained in his appreciation of his innovation, and while there are those who admire its beauty, it is essentially a robust, two-fisted hired hand in the unsentimental world of newspaper production. Despite its popularity, and notwithstanding what seemed a very way-behind-the-curve adoption by the US Department of State in 2004 as a house style for diplomatic documents, on the pages of a newspaper is where it seems best suited. Elsewhere its lack of grace can become apparent. But it never had pretensions to be anything other than a denizen of Fleet Street, and subsequently Wapping, and it is testament to its sound, unfussy design, its authority and sheer presence on the page, that since the arrival of the personal computer so many have felt that for a multitude of purposes it simply looked and felt 'right'.

PEIGNOT

FIRST APPEARANCE   1937, FRANCE
DESIGNER   CASSANDRE (ADOLPHE MOURON), UKRAINIAN

Ukrainian-born Adolphe Mouron, known as Cassandre (1901–1968), designed many of the posters which, for subsequent generations, have come to define Paris in the 1920s and 1930s. His graphic work for railways, cruise liners, cars, clothes, music, sport, drinks and cigarettes seems to sum up modernity and pleasure, as we imagine it to have been in interwar Paris, drawing on Futurist and Surrealist influences to create truly monumental advertising art – with the stress on art. One of his most celebrated designs is the sequence of a man drinking Dubonnet, who turns from line drawing to full colour under the beneficial influence of the drink. Cassandre was a stupendously talented graphic designer; his logo for Yves Saint Laurent can still be seen at any perfume counter. He also designed several striking typefaces, essentially display faces. His early designs, Bifur and Acier, were block letters with playful twists, decidedly art deco. But it was with 1937's Peignot, named after Charles Peignot, the director of Deberny & Peignot, the Paris foundry which produced it, that he attempted something radically different: a text face based on upper-case forms.

Cassandre's family were prosperous émigrés who, following a move to Paris in 1915, were cut off from their homeland by the 1917 Russian Revolution. Initially embarking on a career as a painter, he studied at three institutions, including the Académie Julian, and seems to have been drawn from an early stage to the poster as a form of creative expression. It has been suggested that his pseudonym was created with a later plan to return to painting under his own name. His son Henri Mouron in his 1985 biography draws a link, however, with his father's recorded opinions and those of the Bauhaus in Germany, of the redundancy of the idea of fine art as a free-standing profession – that its qualities only made sense in the modern world when channelled into the service of craft and industry. Cassandre linked his work with the discipline of architecture, with which the Bauhaus is now perhaps mostly strongly associated in our minds: 'the art I prefer above all others ... and has inspired my love of vast surfaces which are destined by their impersonal bareness to be covered with large publicity frescoes'.

Like the Bauhaus, Cassandre understood the importance of lettering, writing in 1926:

> Unrecognised or underrated by our predecessors for far too long, the letter indeed plays a major role in the poster. It is really the leading actor of the mural scene, since it – and it alone – tells the public the magic formula that sells the product... The primacy of the letter is being asserted with increasing force as time goes by. I take some pride in having contributed within my measure to this development.

Already his work was remarkable not just for the images; lettering was a crucial part of his powerful, geometrical structures. Sometimes it would become at an equal partner; sometimes the dominant one. Where Cassandre took a dia-metrically opposed position to leading German typographic thought was his championing of the upper-case letter. 'I am aware that experimental science has ruled against capitals and in favour of lower-case letters, which are more legible, it claims, than the former', he wrote. 'Nevertheless, I remain unfailingly loyal to upper-case letters. The lower-case is in my opinion merely a manual distortion of the monumental letter – an abbreviation, a cursive alteration introduced by copyists.'

SALOMÉ

SCÈNE

(Une grande terrasse dans le palais d'Hérode donnant sur la salle de festin. Des soldats sont accoudés sur le balcon. A droite il y a un énorme escalier. A gauche, au fond, une ancienne citerne entourée d'un mur de bronze vert. Clair de lune)

Le jeune Syrien. Comme la princesse Salomé est belle ce soir !

Le Page d'Hérodias. Regardez la lune. La lune a l'air très étrange. On dirait une femme qui sort d'un tombeau. Elle ressemble

9

Cassandre seemed to reluctantly concede here that all-capitals was less legible in text than lower case, because of the varied word shapes the latter produced, but, undeterred, proposed to incorporate this quality into Peignot. Sans serif, in its lower case it used upper-case forms for x-height high characters, modified, as in the h, k, l and f, to create ascenders, in the p, g, j and y to form descenders. There were concessions to the minuscule forms in the b and d, and with the dots on the i and j. The overall effect is one of great rhythmic beauty, almost a sans serif 1930s' blackletter in its emphasis on a strong vertical stroke.

But Cassandre was proposing a revolution in the way letterforms were to be regarded, if his design was to be a success. '[T]he history of writing, as we know, tells a story of gradual change, not violence', conceded his son, who also blamed 'the baleful effects of photo-composition' for contributing to the face's failure. He doesn't clarify what these adverse effects were, but he may have been referring to poor letterspacing. Like blackletter, Peignot needs extreme regularity, unrelenting evenness of spacing, to project its full beauty. But it did survive through the photosetting era, appearing in light, medium and bold weights, and was a constant feature in the list of dry-transfer lettering company Letraset.

As a text face it never caught on, and its use has largely been confined to display, precisely what Cassandre was trying to move beyond. It appeared for example as the shirt lettering for the David Beckham-period Real Madrid of the early 2000s. There, as elsewhere, it was handsome, striking, and bearing that distinctive but hard-to-quantify Frenchness which also infuses the work of Roger Excoffon (*see* CALYPSO; ANTIQUE OLIVE). A designer whose graphics were monumental in their effect, Cassandre responded to the monumental in letter design to create an alphabet that is, in its way, a work of genius.

STENCIL

FIRST APPEARANCE 1937, UNITED STATES
DESIGNERS ROBERT HUNTER MIDDLETON, BRITISH/AMERICAN;
GERRY POWELL, AMERICAN

'Type' is defined as letterforms that can be mechanically repeated; the reproduction, variations in quality notwithstanding, of a predetermined letterform design. This is in contrast to letters cut in stone, or drawn by hand. But although it is also created by hand on a letter-by-letter basis, stencilled lettering falls within the boundaries of the definition. The letterform is predetermined, cut out of a thin sheet material such as card, metal or plastic, and the letter can be easily duplicated by the application of ink, paint – by brush or, more usually, an aerosol can – even filled in using pencils. Areas such as counters need to be physically linked to the 'negative space' outside the letter by a part of the stencil sheet itself, which when the image of the letter is created forms a negative isthmus across the positive areas; it is this practical restriction that defines the stencil style.

Although creating typefaces that mimic this effect might seem an inverted kind of logic, the style seems to hold an eternal romance for many graphic designers; for every one that wants to create a seamless world of Swiss-style visual economy, there is another who would like their design to look, with just the slightest sense of self-conscious contrivance, as though it has been found in the street, the work of unknown hands. Stencil styles in type provide an easy way to apply a simulated level of the urgently hand-applied to a design. It brings to mind lettering and numerals on metal or wooden

TEA-CHEST

A STENCIL TYPE

How strange that stencilled letter-forms have had no place in the spate of type designs which in recent years, has descended with such fury upon the unsuspecting printer and typographer. Stencils are certainly available and can be purchased from any shop dealing in artists' materials, but the so-called ease of handling of stencils is an overrated legend (as you will hear from any lettering artist) and the results are scarcely ever satisfactory. This is a pity, for the stencil character, if well-designed has many points in its favour.

Tea-chest is such a character. It is unusual, yet by no means bizarre or illegible. It is condensed, and will bring out those important words in a display with just the exact degree of emphasis. it is as suitable for use in the editorial pages of magazines as it is in the advertisement columns. Tea-chest is as useful for a letterhead as it is for a dust wrapper. Tea-chest is, in short, a display type which will find a ready place in the specification of the typographer and in the repertory of the printer and type-setter.

STEPHENSON BLAKE

STEPHENSON BLAKE & CO LTD · THE CASLON LETTER FOUNDRY · SHEFFIELD

TEA-CHEST, DESIGNED BY ROBERT HARLING FOR STEPHENSON BLAKE, 1939.

commercial packaging and containers, Second World War US Army military supplies, or perhaps vital consignments to Fidel Castro's revolutionary-era Cuba.

Paul Renner's heaviest version of Futura (*see* FUTURA), 1929's Futura Black, is in effect a stencil form. That may have been his intention, or he could equally have been taking the strong vertical strokes of blackletter, or the extreme stroke contrasts of nineteenth-century fat faces, and applying the geometric sensibility he had employed for his ultimately discarded experimental characters in the original Futura designs.

Robert Harling (1910–2008) was a graphic designer who ran his own advertising agency, edited design journals and wrote novels. He designed three faces for the Sheffield-based foundry Stephenson Blake, including a stencil face, 1939's Tea-Chest. A post-war specimen from the company pointed out the advantages of typesetting your stencils (*see* opposite). Tea-Chest was a condensed semi-serif, upper case only – semi-serif in that characters such as C, S and G had none, and on others right-hand serifs were omitted from some strokes.

The stencil style, with undertones of honesty and the ruggedly hand-applied, can lend itself to considerable sophistication too. Sébastien Delobel's Rubal Stencil, designed in 2010 for a new secondary school in Lille in France, also boasting a lower case, used sleek sans serif forms to create an information and signage face that is simultaneously stylish and unfussy.

The classic stencil face, as it inhabits popular imagination, became commercially available in the United States in 1937, two versions, identically named but from different companies, hitting the market almost simultaneously. Scottish émigré Robert Hunter Middleton (1898–1985), director of type design at Chicago's Ludlow Typograph Company, is credited with almost 100 designs. His lack of celebrity compared to Goudy

ABCD
12345

or Benton is attributed to his designs being soundly crafted but following trends rather than innovating. Equally the public face of the company was not as prominent as that of American Type Founders, or Goudy's promotion of his own work and persona, supported by his sometimes conflicting roles as roving typographical consultant (*see* GOUDY OLD STYLE).

In the case of Ludlow's Stencil, Middleton seems to have marginally led the field, but ATF's Stencil, the work of in-house designer Gerry Powell (born 1899), seems to have proved the more popular and enduring. The two designs have much in common, upper case only, with strongly contrasted stroke weights. Middleton's serifs are more angular, weightier in proportion to the overall character. Powell's design is slightly more condensed, and this factor probably gave it the edge. Urgency, insistence, are qualities that motivate a designer to choose stencilled lettering as their style of communication. Condensing a letterform gives greater character depth in relation to the available width space in the design, thereby creating greater visual impact. Sometimes called Stencil Bold, Powell's became a standard in the libraries of photosetters through to the 1980s, and was also available as Letraset rub-down lettering.

SUPER VELOZ

FIRST APPEARANCE   1942, SPAIN
DESIGNER   JOAN TROCHUT, SPANISH/CATALAN

War and conflict have inevitably had an impact on the history of type and the lives of its creators. The disappearance and presumed death of Italian printer, scribe and type designer Ludovico degli Arrighi following the plunder of Rome by the forces of the Holy Roman Emperor in 1527 (*see* ARRIGHI); the imprisonment of Stanley Morison as a conscientious objector in the First World War (*see* TIMES NEW ROMAN); the near-starvation of Jan van Krimpen in occupied Holland in 1945 – these are three examples. The total wars of the twentieth century caused the delay or abandonment of innumerable creative projects. But Super Veloz came into being as a direct result of the Spanish Civil War. Its designer was Joan Trochut (1920–1980), a Barcelona-based printer, designer and writer.

For Spain the years between the world wars, as for much of western and central Europe, were ones of political instability. A republic had been declared in 1931, but in 1936 right-wing nationalist army officers, led by Francisco Franco, crossed from their base in Spanish Morocco to mainland Spain, with the intention of overthrowing the republic, and restoring a society of traditional conservative, Catholic values.

Super Veloz, literally 'super fast', had its origins in the work of Trochut's father, Esteban, who had established himself as a printer in the 1920s. At the Barcelona typefounders Fundación Tipográfica José Iranzo he designed and had produced a set of geometric shapes, the Figuras Geometricas, which could be combined to make patterns and in effect illustrations, taking the idea of the conventional printing decorations, or fleurons, to create forms that evoked more the spirit of constructivism and art deco than that of the eighteenth century. Concerned with the prevailing standards of printing in Spain he published a series of journals under the acronym ADAM, Archivos Documentarios de Arte Moderno (Modern Art Documentary Archives). Both Trochuts contributed articles on typography to ADAM.

The Spanish Civil War ended in 1939 with the victory of Franco's Nationalists and the overthrow of the republic. The country was left in dire economic straits, and business prospects for firms trying to survive and rebuild were bleak. Sourcing and financing materials, new equipment, quality paper, and of course metal type, were all challenges printers faced. In Barcelona and Catalonia in particular, which had resisted Franco until the end of the war, repression and censorship were even more punitive than in the rest of the country.

In response to the situation, and still determined to improve printing standards and creativity, Joan Trochut, helped by his father, and with the earlier Figuras Geometricas in mind, set to work creating an experimental modular type system. Rather than complete individual letters, he devised more than 300 modules that could be combined to make a myriad possibilities for letterforms and decorations.

In the 1990s Trochut's grandson Alex began working with type designer Andreu Balius to produce a digital version of Super Veloz, which was commercially released by Balius's Type Republic in 2004. What the buyer receives is no one alphabet, as such, but seven. Two, Complementos Tres and Rasgos Veloz, are composed entirely of decorative flourishes. The others contain in addition stems and strokes both thin

A PROMOTIONAL BROCHURE FOR SUPER VELOZ, 1940S.

and very heavy, the latter capable of bearing patterns or plain. It takes patience, experimentation and usually some revision to create letters, but if you start with a particular set of stems and consider which will form part of the structures of the required characters, it is not difficult to quickly establish the essential structure to build the word. With imagination the results can be striking; extravagant, plump and sumptuous, Super Veloz invokes the spirit of a southern European creative avant-garde, visual fantasies that run parallel to those of Antoni Gaudí, but brought to the page, drenched in Mediterranean heat.

Unsurprisingly Super Veloz was given an Excellence in Type Design Award by the Type Directors Club of New York in 2005. Now removed from the environment and circumstances which brought it into being, Super Veloz affords arguably only occasional opportunities for use, but remains a remarkable piece of inventive, free-form thinking, testament to its creator's determination to overcome some of the obstacles facing his profession.

HELVETICA

FIRST APPEARANCE   1957, SWITZERLAND
DESIGNERS   MAX MIEDINGER, EDUARD HOFFMANN, SWISS

The ultimate typeface? Certainly the only one to have a feature-length film made about it. Gary Hustwit's *Helvetica* appeared in 2007 and looked at the typeface's history, its presence in the environment, and what designers thought of it. The reactions were extreme, from the face being compared to junk food, to practitioners who used nothing but. Environmentally, what was interesting was that Helvetica was so ubiquitous, yet strangely invisible. It was effective in making you notice and read the words it was forming, but for most people any awareness that a design style was at work would have never registered. It is the typographic incarnation of Beatrice Warde's 'crystal goblet', where the message and not the messenger is paramount.

It is this visual Teflon coating that gives Helvetica its unique character. In a prelapsarian typographic Eden this is how you feel the alphabet would have looked, frolicking with chaste abandon until an upper-case S offered it the fruit of knowledge. By comparison, other letterforms look like suits of clothes put on for a day or night out. Helvetica feels like the alphabet in its absolutely purest form. This is a tribute to the conviction with which all the letterforms are drawn. There are no quirks on any of the characters that catch the eye, that make you say 'that's Helvetica'. There are no weak characters that 'don't quite work' with their companions, that mar the appearance of a word aesthetically, or compromise its legibility.

If there is a good identifying element, it's the curves of the lower case c and e in the medium and bold weights, positive in their horizontal terminals.

Yet there's more to it than that. Helvetica's strength comes not just from the forms of the letters themselves, but from the space around and inside them when they're put together as words. It's about the negative space as well as the positive. This again becomes increasingly apparent in the medium and bold weights, where the balance between those two zones is more equal. It is when you see the letters grouped into words, into sentences, that you recognize Helvetica. It might be argued that to make extended or condensed versions of the face, which of course has been done, is to destroy what made it so effective in the first place.

Like many typefaces, Helvetica's history has some ambiguity. It first appeared in 1957, the product of the Swiss foundry Haas, based in Münchenstein. Eduard Hoffmann, the company's director, wanted to update their existing Haas Grotesk, with a view to exploiting the growing strength and influence of the Swiss, or International, style of graphic design and graphic philosophy. The Swiss school of design had its basis in order, a spirit abroad in design generally in the post-war years. Although 'order' was a word which had acquired sinister connotations under Hitler's Third Reich, it might also bring beneficial results to dislocated populations and ruined nations in the aftermath of the war. This order expressed itself on the page through the grid – pictures and text aligned both horizontally and vertically, sans serif type left aligned, space, simplicity, often a limited colour palette. In the words of leading theorist Josef Müller-Brockmann, the grid was 'the expression of a certain mental attitude inasmuch as it shows that the designer conceives his work in terms that

THE BLACK ITALIC WEIGHT, SEEN IN AN EARLY HAAS SPECIMEN, SHOWS HOW MASTERFULLY HELVETICA DOMINATES THE SPACE ALLOTTED TO IT.

are constructive and oriented to the future… His work should thus be a contribution to general culture and itself form part of it.' Much of the Swiss style was a continuation of styles and theories that had been developing in Germany in the interwar years (*see* FUTURA).

'Grotesque' was a nineteenth-century term for sans serifs, and Haas Grotesk had its roots in the German Akzidenz Grotesk. The drawings for what was originally named Neue (New) Haas Grotesk were made by Max Miedinger (1910–1980). Miedinger was an in-house designer for the company, with a previous type design, Pro Arte, to his name; he has generally been credited solely with the creation of Helvetica. The *Helvetica* film presents Miedinger rather as a former graphic designer who had moved into type sales, believing it to be more profitable, and that, although he may have wielded pen and pencil, Hoffmann had the vision, and made numerous recorded comments and suggestions for improvements in the

THE STUFF THAT SURROUNDS
US: HELVETICA'S BAGGAGE-FREE
AUTHORITY CHANNELLED INTO
CONTEMPORARY IDENTITIES.

characters. Hoffmann's son Alfred, who succeeded him as
director, states that it was an absolute collaboration, as neither
could have done it without the other. Miedinger had no one to
argue his case in the film – but the fact that Hoffmann turned
to him to draw the face suggests he was always more than just
a sales rep.

Haas's parent company was the Frankfurt-based Stempel,
which rechristened the face 'Helvetica', drawing on the Latin
name for Switzerland, 'Helvetia'. It was a runaway success,
and came to typify many areas of design and design thought

in the 1960s and into the following decade. As type designer
Jonathan Hoefler described Helvetica, 'There's something
about it that does have a feeling of finality to it ... the con-
clusion of one line of reasoning was this typeface, and perhaps
everything after it is secondary in some way.'

Some equate the use of Helvetica as redolent of a sinister,
attempted mind-control by big corporations, and of right-wing,
conservative thinking. It was certainly seized on by many
corporations and businesses in the 1960s. It spoke of modernity, of fresh thinking, order and efficiency.

The problem, of course, with human beings is that they
only like order within certain limits. For most people it's an
aspiration, but not a natural state of mind. We all want to
be able to put our hands on our house keys in an instant,
but most of us waste a lot of time over a year looking for
them. It is perhaps not surprising that the 1960s also saw a
taste for what, aesthetically, would be seen as the antithesis of
Helvetica: art nouveau styling and decorative Victoriana.

By contrast to the type styles associated with these
nineteenth-century revivals, most people who are not designers
would fail to ascribe any style to Helvetica at all. And, as a
designer, if you want to use a typeface that seems to carry no
visual baggage or 'tics' around with it, that just communicates
to the reader on both a conscious and a subconscious level
merely its content, then Helvetica is a great choice. 'Like air',
as Hoefler said: an implied criticism perhaps, but also testament to a phenomenal achievement. We're still breathing it in
every day.

CALYPSO

FIRST APPEARANCE   1958, FRANCE
DESIGNER   ROGER EXCOFFON, FRENCH

The type designer Matthew Carter's parachute test, in which you could be dropped into an unknown country and know where you were purely from looking at the typography – a possibility he conceded was now largely non-existent as a result of globalization – still often applies in France, where the presence of Roger Excoffon (1910–1983) looms large even now, through both prominent use of his actual typefaces and those inspired or derived from them. Elsewhere it feels almost as though Excoffon's fonts – Banco, Choc, Mistral, Calypso, Diane and Antique Olive – have reached work-of-art status. It can be hard to use them without notional quotation marks, so distinctive are they, redolent of the era in which they were designed and all the cultural associations that go with it.

Excoffon's type designing was inextricably bound up with the trajectory of the Marseilles-based Fonderie Olive and its rivalry with the Parisian Deberny & Peignot in the immediate post-war years and through the 1950s. The name Olive has associations with printing in Marseilles that date back to the seventeenth century. For the foundry that bore the name, its golden years came about under the guidance of Marcel Olive, who gradually took over management of the company from his father Albert. The year Albert retired, 1940, was a calamitous one for the nation, but for Fonderie Olive the period of German occupation would actually help to create beneficial long-term side effects. France was split in two, the northern and Atlantic coastal areas under direct German control, the centre and south forming the unoccupied zone under the supervision of the collaborationist Vichy government. Given the inability to send type to the south, Deberny & Peignot's market was a vacuum which Fonderie Olive was able to fill.

Himself a native of Marseilles, Excoffon had trained as a lawyer, but to his parents' chagrin had abandoned this career path with a view to being an artist. His position with Fonderie Olive came about through family connections; his sister Geneviève was married to Marcel Olive. Excoffon had endured an uninspired fortnight of experience with the company during the war, but an opportunity in 1945 to direct the Paris office of the company was, he claimed – somewhat improbably, as he was thirty-five at the time – the first paid work he'd ever been offered, and, with a wife and children to consider, he accepted.

Nepotism it may have been, but Marcel had acquired himself a major talent. Tall, thin and elegant, described as – depending on his mood – both glacial and charming, Excoffon must have occasionally been perceived by Deberny & Peignot as some kind of typographic vampire, feeding and nourishing on them and their ideas. The rationale for Excoffon's design directions was sometimes a direct result of the commercial battle with the northern firm, to match and better what they were offering, supported by beautiful and energetic promotional material. In its efforts to do so, Fonderie Olive had, in Excoffon, a superlative creative force at its disposal. His early design Chambord drew criticism for at least spiritual similarities with Cassandre and Charles Peignot's face Touraine, but for his next, Banco, he was even more brazen in his tactics. A photograph had been published of the designer Marcel Jacno working on a new typeface for Deberny. Excoffon took a

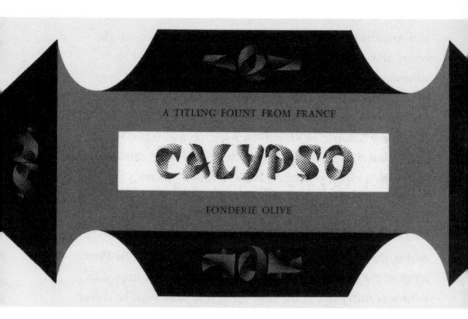

SUPREME ARTISTRY WHICH NEVERTHELESS ALWAYS FOUND ITSELF AT THE LOW-RENT END OF THE MARKET (OPPOSITE).

magnifying glass and studied the picture intently to determine as much as he could of the flavour of Jacno's eponymous work-in-progress, then produced Banco, superior and more commercially successful. Insult was arguably added to injury by the near-anagrammatic nature of Jacno and Banco.

Excoffon built his own distinctive style with script and brush designs like Mistral and Choc, and the heavy pen-strokes of Banco, a kind of blackletter block sans serif, but Calypso was something else again. According to legend, the photographer Richard Blin appeared at the Olive design studio with a photographic enlargement of a halftone dot screen (the process, using dots of varying sizes, by which tonal and colour variation are achieved in printed images) which he had printed. Excoffon's attention was caught by it; he rolled the print into a tube, playing around with it and looking through it. It gave him the idea for an alphabet that was three-dimensional in effect. He recalled: 'Marcel Olive came in and asked me, "Hey what's that?" I told him jokingly, "That's a sketch for a new face of mine." Responding with his usual good business sense, he immediately said "I'll take it."'

The resulting alphabet looked like flat planes covered with a dot screen, curving and twisting in on themselves to form letters. Excoffon claimed that Olive's enthusiasm to produce it was not through any aesthetic motive, but because he believed they were the only foundry capable of successfully producing such a design in metal. Incredibly all the characters were hand-drawn by the design studio, containing grids of white dots on black. With halftones, the smaller the dots become, the more the background dominates, making available through an optical illusion a complete tonal scale from white to black. In Calypso the dots were used to create the illusion of lit and shadowed areas as the planes curved. The new

face was cast in four sizes, unsurprisingly in capitals only.

Calypso could work as a typeface, or as single characters, or could function as pure decoration. It could be regarded as a mid-twentieth-century take on the Victorian decorated letter. When Letraset were considering producing it as dry transfer lettering, Excoffon described it to them as 'more of a technical feat than a significant aesthetic creation'. Although this is a frank and largely accurate assessment, Letraset were nonetheless seduced by the face and took it on board. For it is seductive, against what one might consider one's better judgement. Calypso may indeed not be aesthetically pleasing – although that's a matter of taste, of course – and one can imagine it as the signage for a discotheque somewhere in Europe at any time from the late 1960s through to the 1980s, the sound of Belle Époque's *Black is Black* or Lipps Inc.'s *Funky Town* drifting out through the entrance. For all the skill and technical prowess involved in the making of Calypso, apart from Fonderie Olive's own unfailingly beautiful promotional material, the place where it has customarily been asked to perform has always been the lower end of the market, in terms of style and ambience.

But for sheer élan, for taking all the accepted conventions of how to go about designing a typeface, throwing them out of the window and replacing them with something that grabs the attention and lets it go with the greatest reluctance, while working beautifully within its own terms of reference – and it is above everything else beautifully designed – it has the mark of greatness.

TRANSPORT

FIRST APPEARANCE   1958, GREAT BRITAIN
DESIGNERS   JOCK KINNEIR, BRITISH;
MARGARET CALVERT, SOUTH AFRICAN

Among Beatrice Warde's accomplishments, she was famous for her lecture and subsequent essay 'The Crystal Goblet', in which she stated that the primary requirement of typography – or 'printing' as she termed it – was invisibility (*see* GARAMOND). By this she meant that if the reader noticed the type, be it on account of style, size, weight, line spacing, then it was impeding the task with which it had been entrusted, the smooth transmission of the message from writer to reader. The jewel-encrusted, finely wrought solid gold goblet might be an impressive and valuable item, but it was the crystal wine glass which allowed the connoisseur to appreciate the colour and body of the wine. Similarly, the typeface should only aim to transmit the message with maximum clarity and without interference. Any attention drawn from the reader to the type itself was an unpardonable distraction.

If any classification of typeface needs to conform to the strictures of 'The Crystal Goblet', it is that of road signage. Directional signage in public buildings has a readership that may have time to pause and appreciate its styling in relation to the building and its interiors. Even railway stations or airports can support a little stylistic indulgence, although anyone trying to catch a plane with minutes to spare, searching for their gate in a crowded terminal, will not be in the mood to appreciate typographic niceties. But the lettering on roads and particularly motorways needs to be clear, unambiguous and legible at the maximum distance possible, a distance that is ever decreasing with speed, with the reader making simultaneous physical and interpretive decisions. The typeface needs those qualities and no more. Convenience, schedules, tempers and, as a result, lives may depend upon it.

Britain's road signage typeface, now called Transport, is so much a part of the visual fabric of the country that outside of a car it probably rarely earns a second glance, in part because a lot of its locations don't favour exploration by pedestrians. Nor, of course, has it always been with us, making its first appearance at the end of 1958 on the freshly opened Preston bypass, itself something of a road network guinea pig, an outrider for the first component of the nation's new motorway system which would open the following year, and which would become known as the M1.

The previously incumbent style had been introduced in 1933. Place names were set in black sans serif capitals, in white panels on backgrounds of white, yellow or pale blue. The letters were not particularly large, but this wasn't an issue at the time of their introduction, road usage being comparatively light. Any immediate development was brought to a standstill by the Second World War and the consequent wartime petrol rationing, which didn't end until 1950. But by 1959, the year of the opening of the M1, the British motor industry was producing more than three times the number of vehicles it had in 1938. The economy of the country was noticeably reviving after the prostration of the immediate post-war period; as prime minister Harold Macmillan famously pointed out at the time, 'most of our people have never had it so good'. More of those people could now afford a car and wanted to go places.

TWO OF JOCK KINNEIR AND MARGARET CALVERT'S ORIGINAL 'MAQUETTES'
OF THEIR ROADSIGN DESIGNS.

For the design of the new signage, the Ministry of Transport and Civil Aviation called upon Richard 'Jock' Kinneir (1917–1994). A student at Chelsea College of Art, his career path had been interrupted by the war, but following the end of hostilities he worked in the Design Research Unit of the Central Office of Information. He opened his own design practice in the mid-1950s, while also working part-time as a tutor at his old college. His first big commission arrived in the form of the design of the signage for Gatwick Airport, at this point undergoing major development. To help him he took on one of his former students, Margaret Calvert (born 1936). Together they were to work on many national signage systems.

Although the design of the resulting alphabet came about after research into existing European and United States signage, its superiority in comparison to that still predominant in the USA is swiftly apparent. The latter, popularized by Toby Frere-Jones's digital font Interstate, and known officially as the FHWA series (Federal Highway Administration), was created by engineers and never tested, and is rumoured to have been directly based on the letterforms of a stencil set. The letter-spacing is usually too wide, weakening the impact of the word, a tendency which is exacerbated when using lower-case letters.

Transport, looked at closely, reveals itself to be a solid sans serif, used in upper and lower case, letterspaced slightly wider than it would be on the printed page – wide enough to separate the individual letters at distance, but tight enough to satisfactorily hold the compactness of the word shape. Every letterform is quietly assertive, but emanates an awareness, minutely considered and calibrated, of its relation to its companions. The dot on the i is weighty and sits close, but not too close, to the top of its stem. The tails of the g and y equally don't stray too far from the main body of the character, but make a quiet, distinct statement on their own behalf. The lower finial of the t is hooked and, crucially, so is that of the l, in approved Edward Johnston style.

Looked at out of context Transport may seem an unremarkable, workaday sans serif, but workaday is exactly what it was designed to be. Its beauty comes from how efficiently it performs the task it was created for.

ANTIQUE OLIVE

FIRST APPEARANCE   1960 (NAMED IN 1962), FRANCE
DESIGNER   ROGER EXCOFFON, FRENCH

Although the French designer Roger Excoffon is most closely
associated with bold, highly individual display faces (*see*
CALYPSO), Antique Olive was a determined foray into the
design of a text face. A whole family of weights was produced,
but unusually the face made its first appearance with its
boldest weight. The late 1950s saw the appearance of two major
sans serifs, Helvetica and Adrian Frutiger's Univers. Marcel
Olive, the managing director of Excoffon's employer Fonderie
Olive (*see* CALYPSO), wanted a player in that field from his
company as well. Excoffon's first response was Nord, which
appeared in 1958, an ultra bold weight, most distinctive in its
lower case, its vertical proportion dominated by the x-height.
Ascenders and descenders were short. In the same year, its
slightly modified capitals were used for the new Air France
logo. Nord's success prompted Fonderie Olive to press on with
what would eventually become a full family.

   In his elucidation of the thinking behind what became
Antique Olive (*antique* being the French term for sans serif)
Excoffon made much of the intensive study that had gone into
readability. Referring to an earlier sans serif project, Catsilou,
he spoke of abandoning the viewpoint of the historian for that
of the physicist; rejecting conventional lines of design thinking
in favour of a completely open mind in analysing data about
how letters are read, and applying that research to the new
design.

ABCDEFGHIJKLMNOPQRSTUV
WXYZŒ&1234567890AIÉÈÊË
abcdefghjklmnopqrstuvwx
yzàäbçdéèêëfghiklmnôöpù
c. 48
ABCDEFGHIJKLMNOPQRSTUVWXYZ 12
34567890Æ&ŒABÇDEÉÈÊFGHIKLMNÖ
abcdefghijklmnopqrstuvwxyzœæîû
c. 36
ABCDEFGHIJKLMNOPQRSTUVWXYZ123456789
abcdefghijklmnopqrstuvwxyzàbçdéèmnoü
c. 30

ROGER EXCOFFON'S ORGANIC SANS SERIF, FROM AN EARLY FONDERIE OLIVE SPECIMEN.

What this research indicated was that lower-case words are far easier to still recognize if the descenders are absent than if the ascenders are, that the eye moves along the tops of letters and the x-height to determine the word. For most fonts, other than monoline ones, the stress on curved sections of letters, the thicker sections, will be positioned vertically or at a slight inclination. But Excoffon spoke of a 'shift of weights', and placed his stress at the top of the x-height. This horizontal stress was also subtly used in the upper case for horizontal strokes.

What Excoffon produced was a highly readable sans serif face that was extremely individual, instantly recognizable in a field where many designs bear a close similarity to each other. Sans serifs work within a relatively tightly confined set of parameters, something the American designer Frederic Goudy, for instance, couldn't grasp. He conceded that his half-hearted efforts to design a sans serif were a failure, though possibly not realizing that at least part of his problem was that he thought that sans serifs could bear any features, such as flourishes, as long as there were no serifs on them. Excoffon, however, working within the restrictions that the philosophy of the form demands, managed to produce something highly distinctive, though possibly, and ironically, at the expense of any real chance of lasting success.

Antique Olive, with its large x-height, is highly practical, highly readable, and a precursor of the proportional balance favoured by the International Typeface Corporation (ITC) in the 1970s, which they imposed both on new designs and on the company's restylings of classic faces. Some see, in the shape of the lower-case o, something decidedly olive-like. If not a deliberate homage to the company, it nevertheless suggests an organic feel to the design.

Yet, like Excoffon's other notable designs, it carries heavily the mark of its creator. It is quirky, distinctive and ultimately, perhaps fatally, scene-stealing, having, in the end, too much personality for its essential purpose. A parallel example is Gill Sans, designed to be a text face, yet rarely used as one – again possibly too organic in feeling, a quality that seems to work against sans serifs in this context.

It's a failure, then, in its aim to be a dominant sans serif performer, but a stylish failure. As Sébastien Morlighem asks in *Roger Excoffon and the Fonderie Olive* (2010), 'Is Antique Olive recognised today ... for its principles of legibility? Or because it embodies, to the same extent as Excoffon's other designs, a certain typographic aura "à la française" that exerts a lasting fascination?'

DATA 70

FIRST APPEARANCE 1971, GREAT BRITAIN
DESIGNER BOB NEWMAN, BRITISH

'The future isn't what it used to be', says Robert De Niro's Lucifer in the film *Angel Heart*. It's a good line, and one that comes to mind when considering the qualities of Data 70. It has come to symbolize the future as seen from a late 1960s or early 1970s perspective; a future dominated by computer technology in a way that people could only imagine, but one that looked, despite some elements of depersonalization, essentially glamorous, a price worth paying for the loss of the sometimes irksome demands of individuality. It would be a future of the unisex, zippered catsuit, of airborne personal transporters, possibly matter dematerialization and reassembly, and nourishment taken solely in pill or liquid form. Disease and illness would have been eradicated; war, apart from – possibly – with extraterrestrial life forms, was no more. There would be racial harmony. There would be no need to ever feel depressed, or even slightly low.

The appearance of Data 70 in the Letraset range in 1971 has been the cause of mild resentment ever since. Leo Maggs was a designer working in the early 1960s for the Hazell Sun Group, based in London's Covent Garden. One of his employer's regular projects was to design the magazine for the Friends of Covent Garden Opera House. Maggs was asked to draw a piece of 'futuristic' lettering for the headline of one of the magazine's articles, which he based on the MICR (Magnetic Ink Character Recognition) numerals found at the bottom

ABCDEFGHIJKL MNOPQRSTUV WXYZ abcdefghij klmnopqrstuvwxy z 1234567890 &?!BE$[:]

Data 70

FUTURISTIC STYLE FROM THE 1970S.

of bank cheques, which detail the cheque number, the bank sort code and the account number. MICR contains only the ten numerals plus four special symbols. Their salient physical feature is a combination, in places, of highly contrasting thin and thick strokes, but with the contrast styled in a way Giambattista Bodoni would not have recognized – where it occurred, it was contained within the stroke itself, in a sudden, stepped progression.

It was this characteristic that Maggs threaded throughout the letters for his headline, and then into the complete alphabet that he developed in about 1965. The only diagonals in the design were contained in those steps, an angled progression from one stroke thickness to another, and in a sole instance, in the dog-legged, right-hand stroke of the V, both upper and lower case.

He offered the design to dry-transfer lettering company Letraset, who rejected it as insufficiently commercial, following which it was taken up by the photosetters Photoscript, who christened it Westminster, presumably after the National Westminster Bank. The face's most high profile appearance was in the titles and credits of the 1968 film *Sebastian*, starring Dirk Bogarde and Susannah York.

Much to Maggs's chagrin, in 1971 Letraset now judged Westminster's stylistic terrain to be a more profitable one, and released Data 70, the design of which is credited to Letraset studio man Bob Newman – although it is uncertain whether his role was as the conceptual originator, or simply as the person who physically drew the characters. Data 70's inception, like many of Letraset's originals, would have come about as the result of a committee-based decision, in this instance to fill a perceived gap in the market for a futuristic face, a gap they had already explored successfully with Colin Brignall's Countdown, released in 1969.

Data 70 was in essence remarkably similar to Westminster, although it could be argued that anyone looking at MICR for inspiration would have arrived at some similar conclusions. Data 70 was more condensed – Westminster was based on the wider proportions of Gill Sans – and is arguably a sleeker, better accentuated design, with the concept more elegantly and consistently applied throughout.

The move paid off for Letraset; they had produced a design that managed to encapsulate what people thought about a certain thing at a certain period in time. Looking at it now brings to mind 1970s television programmes like *The Tomorrow People* or *Space 1999*, regardless of whether it was actually used by them or not, and the covers of innumerable mass-market paperbacks, either science fiction or purporting to be science fact. To use it now would be to place metaphorical quotation marks around the words in question, and the overall design. But that only serves to emphasize how perfectly Data 70 was of its time, for its time, if not for any other. It is still available as a digital font. Westminster was sold in 1993 to Microsoft at the instigation of Robert Norton, the former owner of Photoscript.

BLOODY HELL

FIRST APPEARANCE   MID-1970S, GREAT BRITAIN
DESIGNER   UNKNOWN

Sometimes there can be a beautiful directness in a typeface
that seeks to capture just one mood, one idea, that completely
ignores the rule that type should be stylistically invisible, so
as not to interfere with the message, and creates an alphabet
that is a narrative in itself, yet doesn't take itself seriously for a
moment. Bloody Hell, and similar faces of different name but
exactly the same concept, sought to evoke the world of 1940s
and 1950s low-budget horror as presented in pulp novels or
cinema, an essentially hand-drawn form in which the formal-
ity of the letters is broken and they appear to be melting, or
dripping with blood.

There have always been novelty typefaces. But ideas such as
making alphabets out of gymnastic polar bears – it happened
– or nude women – of course it happened, more than once –
are illustrations mimicking letterforms. Sticking smiley faces
on each character, or for each to contain an illustration of
sunrise over the pyramids (both of which styles have also been
commercially available) are bolted-on ideas. Bloody Hell and
its variants are something different. They take the letterforms
themselves and envisage a transformation, a change of state, a
melting, an extrusion of innards, or the consequences of the
letterforms coming into contact with another element, some
sort of viscous liquid. The letters have begun as unadulterated
forms, but, with no additions being made, no illustrative
elements, no drop shadows, no illusion of the third dimension

Bloody Hell ©

ABCDEFGHIJKLM
NOPQRSTUVWXYZ
abcdefghijklmnopqrstu
wxyz£1234567890$
&(.,`'!?)

IF THE DIRECTIONAL SIGNAGE TO CASTLE DRACULA WASN'T SET IN BLOODY
HELL, IT SHOULD HAVE BEEN.

added, they have changed. It's a simple, but effective idea.
Cheap possibly, but powerful and memorable, and inherently
pure as a concept. The result can invoke unease, or can make
you smile, a difficult combination to carry off.

Probably because the style was one that could be fairly
easily created by hand, perhaps by customizing and embellish-
ing an existing face, commercially offered variants are fewer
than memory might suggest. Letraset seem to have steered
clear. Among photosetting companies of the 1970s and 1980s,
London-based Conways', who claimed to have the largest collection of headline faces in the country, offered a ragged, heavy
block letter called Frankenstein's Bride, and a genuine 'dripper'
called, perhaps inevitably, Dracula. The prize for getting properly behind the style may well go to a phototypesetter of the

same period, Alphabet, who actually had two versions, Bloody Horror, a melting or dripping bold roman with soft, rounded serifs, and Bloody Hell, given a further lift, an illusion of the third dimension if required, by having highlights on the drips.

The style survives in the digital age; as just one example, the site dafont.com has numerous variants in the horror subsection of its 'Fancy' division, some absorbing and channelling grunge influences from the 1990s. The relative lack of overheads in creating a digital font has meant niche ideas can be more fully explored, and here they've been explored fully. With the continuing popularity of horror as a genre, coupled with the reawakened interest in the early twenty-first century with the hand-drawn, it's an area that was ripe for development. Amid the scratchy, pen- and brush-based forms, and the splatters, it's reassuring to see that melting and dripping letterforms remain a standard.

In recent years Hollywood horror has frequently used the industry go-to font, Carol Twombly's Trajan, a sleek and imposing re-creation of Roman inscriptional lettering, to present both terror and romantic comedy, and all points in between. But that doesn't mean the films were better. Let's be honest about what's being presented in a genre that may sometimes drop below the cultural radar, but never goes away. Just occasionally, let those titles drip.

ARCADIA

FIRST APPEARANCE   1986, GREAT BRITAIN
DESIGNER   NEVILLE BRODY, BRITISH

Britain in the early 1980s was a challenging business climate. The country had been in recession since the start of the decade. Failing or underperforming industries were being allowed to go to the wall by the incumbent Conservative government headed by Margaret Thatcher, with unemployment rising at an alarming rate. But, despite this abandonment of many traditional industries, the economy experienced a gradual recovery and a brief, giddy period of consumerism and excess in the second half of the decade. Running parallel to this was a renewed interest in graphic design and typography.

A small spark of brightness in the depressing economic landscape of Britain in the early 1980s was the monthly music and style magazine *The Face*. The creation of former *New Musical Express* editor Nick Logan, *The Face* had launched in May 1980. Unlike the *NME* and similar music titles, *The Face* was not a newspaper format, but a magazine, with better-quality paper, stapled binding and with colour on the cover and on some of the inside pages. Initially styling itself as 'Rock's Final Frontier', its page design was largely unremarkable, with unassertive sans serif headlines.

In August 1981 the name Neville Brody appeared in the design section of the masthead. A recent graduate of the London College of Printing, Brody had been working as a freelance graphic designer in the music industry. His effect on the magazine was gradual, but by late 1982 the graphic

avanti

ARENA

COMPILED BY STEVE TAYLOR, MICHAEL WATTS

STUDIO PHOTOGRAPHY DAVIES & STARR

STRONGER *VODKAS* . . . NEW LOOK *BETTING SHOPS* . . . MATTHEW HILTON'S *TUBULAR FURNITURE* . . . *PAUL SMITH* IN PARIS . . . THE MICRO-*CAMERA* CHUNKY TYROLEAN FOOTWEAR . . . *SWISS ARMY KNIVES* . . . THE ELECTRONIC *ORGANISER* . . .

A SITE-SPECIFIC FONT FOR *ARENA* MAGAZINE, HERE HEADING UP THE AVANTI SECTION OF DESIRABLE LIFESTYLE ACCESSORIES FOR THE MODERN MAN FOR WINTER 1986/87.

style was becoming more individual, structured and playful; elements of postmodernism were creeping in – blocks of colour, spots, geometric devices. Different typefaces were used within a single word. Extremely wide letterspacing, to facilitate different levels of typographic emphasis or purely for style, became a regular feature. Then the typefaces themselves began to change, with Brody beginning to draw his own angular, condensed characters for use in *The Face*'s headlines. The effect at first may have been subliminal. But linked to the increased presence of fashion in the magazine's visual content, and an editorial bias towards musicians who wished to express themselves visually as well as sonically, fuelled by the growing medium of the promotional music video, *The Face* began to be labelled by other sections of the press, with increasing envy of its success and influence, as a 'style bible'.

By the end of the decade, the words 'style' and 'designer' would be competitors for the most unthinkingly and lazily overused words of the 1980s. *The Face* epitomized the growing obsession with those terms of presentation. Brody's graphic style became imitated to the point where it became a cliché. He was given his own exhibition at the V&A museum in 1988, with an accompanying book. Graphic design in Britain was now sexy in a way it had not been before, for prospective art students no longer the workaday play-safe poorer relation to the glamour and danger of fine art and fashion. If it is an exaggeration to say that the popularity of graphic design courses today is largely attributable to Brody and his work and influence, then it is only a mild distortion of the truth.

By 1986, with the economy of the country growing again after the recession, a mood of materialism and conspicuous consumption began to be noticeable. It was during this period that the wealth and the presence of those working the stock markets in the City of London began to make themselves felt. Stockbrokers were no longer perceived as dull middle-aged men in bowler hats, but young, acquisitive and confident, sometimes circumventing the conventional route of university education to achieve unimagined fortune by working in the trading rooms. And they had money to spend.

In response to this prevailing mood in at least the southern half of the country, Nick Logan launched a second publication, *Arena*, which appeared at the end of 1986. It was subtitled *A New Magazine for Men*, a bold leap into an area of publishing long considered a graveyard – a general-interest magazine for a male readership, which wasn't pornographic. With a male cover star, *Arena*'s fashion coverage was of established or emerging expensive labels like Armani, far away from *The Face*'s do-it-yourself art-school-graduate roots, accompanied by reassuringly costly symbols of status and taste – watches, razors, cameras, 'designer' beers and spirits.

Brody had expressed a desire to escape from the styling of *The Face* and return to Helvetica, but *Arena* was graced – used necessarily sparingly – by a new Brody face, later to be called Arcadia. Extremely condensed, with huge x-height and stubby ascenders and descenders, it might best be described as a semi-serif modern – extreme stroke weight contrast, but the serifs never appearing quite where you might conventionally expect them. Most effective used large, black on white or white on black, Arcadia had all the extravagance, beauty and drama of art nouveau or deco lettering, with both curves and angularity, while owing nothing to either of them. Nor did it seem particularly a product of its own time, looking more like something Giambattista Bodoni might have created if he had been catapulted forward a couple of centuries. According to websites selling Arcadia, it was inspired by IBM golfball typewriter faces, but if so it's a visual leap.

Brody's type designs were much imitated by the late 1980s, but the originals themselves were subsequently difficult to use when made commercially available. Brody's designs were highly distinctive, but also site-specific, in that they were seen in magazines like *The Face* and *Arena* that had themselves, because of Brody's input, extremely vibrant visual identities. Perhaps with the passage of time, Arcadia can now stand clear of its original association, and be appreciated and used solely on its merits, as a truly striking, original and beautiful design.

MASON

FIRST APPEARANCE   1992, GREAT BRITAIN

DESIGNER   JONATHAN BARNBROOK, BRITISH

Jonathan Barnbrook (born 1966) is one of Britain's most high-profile graphic designers of the last twenty years. A graduate of two of London's top art colleges, Central St Martins and the Royal College of Art, he was something of a design star even before he graduated. This kind of status, and the individualistic thinking that is needed to attain it, doesn't necessarily translate into immediate employment in the service of others. Work was in short supply during the months after leaving the Royal College. He had originally seen his font designs as purely for his personal use, but changed his mind and approached Émigré, the design magazine and font foundry, who accepted some of them. Among these was Mason, designed in 1992, which was originally called Manson, until it provoked a torrent of complaints: 'I was really surprised when people complained – it [was] called Manson because of the sound of the word', he told *Eye* magazine in 1994.

> It sounds elegant: elegant typeface, elegant name. But then, hopefully, you do a double-take, you think, Manson, where does that come from? He's a mass-murderer. It wasn't that I think Charles Manson is great, or that I wanted to glorify someone who murdered people. I was trying to make you … consider its context differently. … It was designed in Britain, and two or three years ago a lot of British people hadn't really heard of Charles Manson.

The font's name was changed to Mason, much to Barnbrook's dissatisfaction. This sense of a loss of control spurred him to create his own font company, Virus. Despite pronouncing himself sceptical about graphic design's role in servicing 'a capitalist system geared towards production for profit rather than for need', he defended his work in advertising by claiming it to be a medium for furthering people's fantasies or helping them to have them: 'Everyone needs some kind of fantasy and theatre in their life, and advertising is part of that.'

It also generated money that allowed him to spend time designing typefaces, or working on other personal projects. Barnbrook's 'late-twentieth century font catalogue' for his Virus foundry described and illustrated the wares on offer as no type specimen had ever done before. 'Simple steps to a life of spiritual and material gain' announced the cover. The font Drone was described as 'for text without content', Nixon as 'the typeface to tell lies in', False Idol as 'based on the bad rubdown lettering often seen in pornographic magazines'.

Of course, once a designer makes their type generally available, it is impossible to control how it is used. Ironically Barnbrook's blackletter, Bastard, 'to be used by corporate fascists everywhere', found an entirely different appropriation. In October 2011 the Occupy London protest against global economic inequality created a tiny city within a city on a site outside St Paul's Cathedral, until dismantled and dispersed by bailiffs and police in February of the following year. But during that time the camp had produced its own newspaper, *The Occupied Times*, which used Bastard for its title-piece and elsewhere. Barnbrook would no doubt have approved, nonetheless.

Mason appeared at the start of what would become a golden period for typography, its digital age, and represented both a respect for tradition and a breakout from it. Mason works most successfully in its serif version. Embedded in a formal, more classical clothing, characters like the 'cross' T

AMT
WQI
HOQ
MAZ

WHETHER CHRISTIAN OR PAGAN, SUBSTANCE OR MERELY STYLE, IT'S
BEAUTIFULLY DRAWN.

and the alternate, vertically tailed Q, the gothic-arch curved apex of the A and its reverse in the W, become much more sophisticated as designs with their variations in stroke and curve widths. Alternate versions of M both suggest some kind of collapsing Roman temple. The tail of the Regular version of the Q, and of the legs of K and R, are extravagant, sweeping.

Mason's appeal lies in its eccentricity, its feeling of coming from left field and its use of the cross form as an intimation that there is some deeper meaning or signifiers buried within it. It's unsurprising that it got taken up for use in record company graphics, or anywhere where the idea of some kind of spiritual or philosophical unconventionality was to be expressed. But, beyond this, what made it such a success was that it was so beautifully drawn. The photosetting era had seen lots of one-off type designs from individual graphic designers that attempted to break free of existing typographic styles, but often weren't particularly well realized. Mason channelled the elegance of Garamond or Centaur, competed with them on their own terms, and then took itself somewhere else in terms of mood and implied reference points.

As Barnbrook said of his work in the mid-1990s: 'It's only graphic design, which, like pop music, is very ephemeral, yet it is important at the same time.' What, stylistically does Mason seem to be saying? It might be argued that it makes the user and viewer think of religion, but whether it's Christian or pagan, or a mixture of both, is impossible to say. Is it a triumph of style over substance? Perhaps, but if so it's a glorious one. It's about applying your own meaning, using the typeface to suggest and project that meaning, a decidedly postmodern visual empowerment.

NATWEST

FIRST APPEARANCE   1993, GREAT BRITAIN

DESIGNERS   FREDA SACK AND DAVID QUAY, BRITISH

Margaret Thatcher's tenure as prime minister of Great Britain, from 1979 to 1990, saw a radical change in the structure of the nation's economy. In the 1980s, many underperforming traditional industries were allowed to decline, with a shift in emphasis to a service-based economy, particularly financial services. As new laws passed by the government increased competition in the financial markets in London, one outcome was an emphasis on the importance of corporate communication in a fiercely competitive 'free market' economy.

Along with deregulation in the City of London, the 1980s saw a huge rise in the availability of loans to bank customers. The traditional image of the bank manager as a distant, disapprovingly paternal figure, refusing credit for one's own good, disappeared as the decade advanced. Money for mortgage applications could not now, it seemed, be lent quickly enough, occasionally even to applicants with no actual verification of the income necessary to service such a loan. It was a climate unthinkable even in the early years of the decade. Symbolic of this change was the radical redesign of the Midland Bank's Oxford Street branch. The Midland, subsequently bought in the 1990s by HSBC, was one of the traditional 'Big Four' clearing banks. In Oxford Street it made an unequivocal statement, a visual configuration of the spirit of the times: gone were the grey stone columns and classical, Greco-Roman style of banking architecture, replaced with glass, plastic, colour and informality. 'Now we are friendly' was the message; 'come on in.'

Despite another recession at the end of the decade to mirror the one at the beginning, the financial industry continued to evolve. The 1990s saw a series of demutualizations of what had been building societies, their members voting to convert them to bank status, most induced by the offer of free shares or cash payments. The field was more competitive, these new players bringing with them an image of informality and modernity. Another member of the Big Four, the National Westminster Bank, now decided to respond visually to this new climate.

Working with the bank's design consultancy, Wolff Olins, Freda Sack and David Quay were initially asked to design a one-weight serif headline face for the bank, whose existing font palette had been Helvetica, Garamond and Bembo. The new face would be used in newspaper and magazine advertising to create a strong, recognizable image for the National Westminster, and for its strapline, 'We're here to make life easier'. Conceptually speaking, the bank's executives were in adventurous mood. As Freda Sack recalled,

> They were surprisingly open to new ideas – so much so that I feared they were in danger of going too far, and moving away from what would be perceived as acceptable for a bank in terms of a safe and trustworthy identity. We designed a very radical ampersand almost as a protest – but they liked it and it stayed in.

It was one of the first identities that was type-led. The type would be reversed out of a solid background colour, and the audience would be able to recognize the bank's information purely by the font. The proposed design was received extremely positively, to the extent that the limitations of the brief were thrown aside, and the single font was developed into a

Travel services

Banking services

Savings & investments

Mortgages

Pensions & life assurance

Small business services

IF OSCAR WILDE HAD REAPPEARED IN THE 1990S TO TRY HIS LUCK IN
MORE TOLERANT TIMES, THIS MIGHT HAVE BEEN THE TYPEFACE ON HIS
CHEQUEBOOK.

family; a complete rebrand was now afoot. Such was the visual resonance of the design, the implication of a new philosophy abroad in the bank, that National Westminster officially adopted its long-standing vernacular nomenclature 'NatWest'. The message was clear: they too could be friendly, informal even, when needed. It was also the name by which the designers always referred to the fonts. There had never been an official name assigned, perhaps because they had started as such a small element in the original design brief.

A design for the 1990s, with a decided air of playful post-modernism, the serif version of NatWest also strangely evoked the 1890s, formal enough to serve the purposes of a financial institution, but on closer inspection seeming almost to dance across the page, imbued with a sinuous hand-drawn quality that brings to mind the organic nature of art nouveau. If Oscar Wilde had reappeared in the 1990s to try his luck in more tolerant times, this would have been the typeface on his chequebook. Strictly speaking, the serif was in reality a semi-serif; many characters possessed only one such feature, rather than the conventional three or five. The uppercase T, M and W, for example, boasted only one serif each, at top left – but even here there was no uniformity. On the T the serif pointed down, on the M to the left, on the W it was positioned on the inside of the stroke, like a plant's young leaves making their own way towards the sun. By contrast the capital S had no serifs at all. Descenders on the lower case, and the lower terminal of the t, resembled the tails of small dogs, ready at any moment to wag.

The first sans version of NatWest came about through the need for the type family to work at even very small sizes on all the bank's forms and leaflets, such as the Terms and Conditions text, the 'small print'. When the font was reappraised in 1996, Sack and Quay suggested modifying its 'many post-modernist mannerisms', simplifying it, and moving towards a sans serif, which had been one of their original ideas, to 'create a purer, more classic look with a lasting quality – a typeface to take the bank into the new century'. The sans serif version was more solid in feel, less quirky, the upper case with squarer stroke terminals, yet still retaining much of the energy of the earlier incarnation, particularly in the descenders.

Although the bank changed design consultancies over the twenty-year life of the fonts, such was the value placed on them that Sack and Quay were always brought in as type consultants and developers. In 2014 NatWest the bank abandoned NatWest the font in favour of a far more anonymous sans serif as part of a wider brand amalgamation with its owner, the Royal Bank of Scotland. Since the financial crisis of 2008, and some unwelcome stories in respect to the dealings of RBS, the underlying message of NatWest's public image and advertising is 'no tricks, no unfair charges, we are what we seem, you can trust us'. Perhaps the present, more anonymous font is also seen as part of this. But Sack and Quay's designs stand out as truly unprecedented, distinctive corporate faces, oozing character and personality in a field where so much is uniform and ultimately bland. They brightened many an otherwise disheartening bank statement.

COMIC SANS

FIRST APPEARANCE 1995, UNITED STATES
DESIGNER VINCENT CONNARE, AMERICAN

Typographically, Comic Sans occupies a similar cultural position to Cloister Black/Old English (*see* CLOISTER BLACK). The world beyond that of graphic designers and typographers has seized it and placed its own meaning upon it, quite irrespective of what designers believe it signifies or how it should be used. Comic Sans has provoked more vituperation than any typeface in history, with websites dedicated to its eradication and insults fired at its creator. Anything that provokes that sort of reaction clearly has something going for it.

Born in Boston, Massachusetts, Vincent Connare studied fine art and photography at the New York Institute of Technology; he was working as a photographer for Massachusetts newspaper *The Worcester Telegram* when his girlfriend drew his attention to her employers' (the type company Compugraphic) current need for new staff to convert their existing type library, at that point still based in photosetting technology, into digital versions. From there Connare moved in 1993 to Microsoft, working as what he describes as a typographic engineer on faces such as Arial and Matthew Carter's Tahoma. In 1995 he designed the Windows stalwart Trebuchet, and Comic Sans.

Connare saw a developmental version of Microsoft's new interactive program called Microsoft Bob. Cartoon avatars moved from room to room, and conversed using speech bubbles. Visually the problem was that the font used in the bubbles was Times. To a comic book and graphic novel enthusiast like Connare, this just didn't look right. The lettering used in speech bubbles for American comic publishers such as Marvel and DC had clarity and a sense of formal structure, yet exuded an energy through being carefully handwritten. It was nearly always upper case, although there was a precedent in DC's *Watchmen* for lower case, used in 'thought' bubbles. It was this overall style and feeling that Connare was looking to emulate for Comic Sans. He designed a lower case as well – a crucial, or, its decriers would say, fatal decision. Without it the rise of Comic Sans would never have taken place, its absence ruling out use of the font for text. But Comic Sans was only ever designed for one specific use – speech bubbles.

Time constraints meant that it could not be included in Bob, but Microsoft's Consumer Division liked what Connare was doing, so he carried on developing the font, and it first saw daylight in the Microsoft Plus Pack for Windows 95, which had games, sounds and Internet Explorer. It was included in a suite of fonts for a downloadable version of Explorer, and was also shipped with the Windows 95 OEM (original equipment manufacturer) version. This was sold to the hardware producers, who would then customize the operating system and install it in their PCs. With the almost total market dominance of the PC in the 1990s, Comic Sans was suddenly in every office, and in most homes that boasted a computer.

But what happened to make it the world's favourite font? As people ran their eye down the list of available fonts on their computer, what was it about Comic Sans that attracted them? In Connare's words,

> You have to ask, seeing as how you get about 200 free fonts with a new computer, why do people keep picking Comic Sans? ... I've been working at Dalton Maag in London, and we make fonts – fonts for corporations. We get lots of

requests for 'friendly' designs. Companies want to appear warm and friendly so their customers are comfortable using their services.

As he has observed, it looks like the kind of typeface that you wouldn't use to write a letter. It's informal, it's unpretentious, it's friendly; the bold weight looks like something you would have written with a marker pen on the front of a large envelope. These are undoubtedly the qualities that attracted its first users, and made subsequent adopters, seeing it in use, want it too. They must have been delighted to find it had been sitting on their PC all the time, just waiting for them.

The Internet, although facilitating choice and offering easily accessible alternatives, sometimes results in 'winner takes all' situations – search engines and social networks are two examples. One provider comes out on top, eventually sucking up its rivals' users. The explanation proffered for this is that human beings, given choice, will move in substantial numbers towards the same option. Choice, much as we crave it, is in reality somewhat alarming. What if we make the wrong decision? We'll have to live with our folly, while everybody else is riding high. So we tend to look at what others are doing and follow suit. There is comfort in numbers and we have been freed, as we see it, from bearing the consequences of our own decisions.

The ubiquity of Comic Sans has come about largely through a similar process. The non-designer or typographer faced with the question of which font to choose for a document that other people will see can understandably feel paralysed by the terror of making an uninformed decision. It's a potential minefield. So what's everyone else using?

Beyond aesthetic considerations, the opponents of Comic Sans base their objections on the face's inappropriate use. In the mind of its creator, it only had one, and arguably that's the

UTERINE
KIDNEY
APPENDIX
SARCOMA
LYMPHOMA
LIVER
OVARIAN
PROSTATE
TESTICULAR
STOMACH
COLON
PANCREATIC
BREAST

Comic Sans For Cancer

bunchdesign.com

BUNCH DESIGN'S CONTRIBUTION TO 'COMIC SANS FOR CANCER', A 2015
FUNDRAISING EXHIBITION ON THE OCCASION OF THE FONT'S TWENTIETH
BIRTHDAY.

one place we never see it used. As well as text, it can be seen almost everywhere, most discordantly in warning signs, where its amiable, curved forms are wildly, even dangerously, unsuitable: your car will be clamped if you park here; stand well clear of winching equipment. It has even been suggested that organizations with information they are legally required to give us but would prefer we didn't notice use it to slip things past us, the information equivalent of the wolf in sheep's clothing.

Conspiracy theories aside, more than ten years after its rise to global prominence, Comic Sans still provokes its share of online abuse. One particular posting, dating from 2013, is composed of the kind of enraged invective we used to associate with 'Angry of Tunbridge Wells', turned up several notches in intensity, peppered with expletives and drenched in contempt for what the writer sees as the almost criminal stupidity of his fellow man. It's a tone that's depressingly all too familiar to online readers. One user group that incurs his specific wrath is teachers who justify the font as approachable and readable, particularly for young children, but then use it for senior-level communications as well. His other great objection is that Comic Sans is badly designed. Some of the lower-case characters are short on grace at large sizes, but in its designer's defence he only ever intended it to be used at about 8-point size, nearly always in capitals, and black text on white – not, for instance, four or five inches high on signage, in yellow upper and lower case on a blue background. Whatever its shortcomings, it's not going to go away in the near future, and if it does will probably be supplanted by something that has a similar informal feel.

And how wealthy did the world's favourite typeface make Vincent Connare? His payment was his Microsoft salary. 'There was no royalty arrangement – I wish there had been. I'd be richer than Bill Gates!'

AMANAR

FIRST APPEARANCE   2003, FRANCE
DESIGNER   PIERRE DI SCIULLO, FRENCH

There are currently some 7,000 languages in use in the world; a startlingly number perhaps but, taking a historical average, it is calculated that a language disappears about every four months. Linguists predict that by the end of the twenty-first century possibly half of this overall total will exist only as archive recordings, if they are preserved at all. Does this really matter? Aren't there enough languages already? Even perhaps too many? Surely they merely obstruct the perpetually challenged arena of international human understanding?

Judith Thurman, in 'A Loss for Words', her 2015 *New Yorker* article on endangered languages, quotes linguist Daniel Kaufman:

> Let's be honest... The loss of these languages doesn't matter much to the bulk of humanity, but the standard for assessing the worth or benefit of a language shouldn't rest with outsiders, who are typically white and Western. It's an issue of the speakers' perceived self-worth.

She points out that 'the loss of languages passed down for millennia, along with their unique arts and cosmologies, may have consequences that won't be understood until it is too late to reverse them.' An example she gives of concrete global benefit has been the identification of medical properties in plants where the indigenous languages have a far greater, subtler vocabulary in these specialized areas than the dominant language of the region.

Thurman's is a perceptive observation, and surely any initiative to help preserve a language must therefore be applauded. One obvious way to do this, with those languages on the borderline of extinction, is to increase the number of speakers, crucially among young people. Although bilingualism is vital to prevent the speakers from becoming isolated from the wider communities in which, nationally, they live, these indigenous languages can provide a wider sense of identity and self-esteem for a community. A further step is to address the written language. In the digital age, societies have become epistolary once again. For decades the telephone seemed likely to bring an end to personal written communication, but it has been revitalized, albeit in a different form and using different styles and structures of language, by email, Twitter, Facebook, blogs, even by abusive arguments on YouTube. Give an endangered 'outsider' language the means to engage with and use digital media and it becomes open to the possibilities of greatly extended usage, particularly by the younger speakers who are vital for keeping it alive and for passing it on to their own children.

The Tuareg are nomadic people who live in the inner regions of the Sahara desert in North Africa. Though their numbers are estimated at only about 1.2 million, they inhabit a vast area which covers much of southern Algeria, large portions of Niger and Mali, and parts of Libya, Burkina Faso and northern Nigeria. It was and continues to be a lifestyle that comes into confrontation with the governments of these territories. During the period of European colonial expansion in the nineteenth and the first half of the twentieth centuries this was the French. But there have been sporadic outbreaks of conflict between the Tuareg and government forces in Mali and Niger in the 1990s and early twenty-first century. The nomadic existence, crossing as it does national boundaries, is

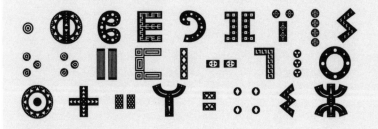

AMANAR, THE HITHERTO PURELY HANDWRITTEN LANGUAGE OF THE TUAREG,
REALIZED IN DIGITAL FORM.

under constant pressure, and some Tuareg have abandoned the herding of animals, which is intrinsic to the culture, to farm or even to forgo the way of life altogether and look for urban employment.

The Tuareg language is known by its speakers variously as Tamajaq, Tamasheq or Tamahaq, depending on region. The French priest Charles de Foucauld (1858–1916) lived among the Tuareg and compiled a dictionary for the language. It remained a handwritten language until the 1990s, when French designer Pierre Di Sciullo (born 1961) began working on a digital version of the Tamajaq alphabet, which culminated in Amanar in 2003.

As well as allowing the Tuareg to use their language and script in conjunction with modern technology, Di Sciullo's design is beautiful in its own right. With all traces of hand-drawn forms removed, the result looks like a series of highly vibrant pictograms, heavily based upon what would be simple mark-marking forms: the circle, the cross, the dot, the stroke. It comes in medium, black, condensed weights, and an inline 'Decor' version, and is available as a free download.

CHANNEL 4 FONTS

FIRST APPEARANCE   HEADLINE: 2005, GREAT BRITAIN
HORSEFERRY: 2015, GREAT BRITAIN
DESIGNER   HEADLINE: JASON SMITH, BRITISH
HORSEFERRY: NEVILLE BRODY, BRITISH

The arrival of Britain's fourth television channel in November
1982 came as a welcome piece of cultural uplift in a year that
had been, for the most part, unrelentingly bleak. Finishing its
BBC run in the same week as Channel 4 launched was Alan
Bleasdale's award-winning drama series *Boys from the Black-
stuff.* Although streaked with flashes of dark humour, the series
was era-defining, a searing reaction to the combined effects of
recession and the policies of Margaret Thatcher's Conservative
government, seemingly unconcerned over the spiralling unemployment the country was experiencing.

It was not a propitious time for the arrival of the nation's
long-contemplated second commercial channel, and for a while
its continuing existence looked far from assured. It was a commercial channel, but advertisers were in extremely short supply,
the channel's early client roster seeming at times to consist
solely of two rival brands of kitchen appliances for chopping
and blending, their advertisements appearing with monotonous
regularity, interspersed with exhortations to others to advertise.
For a while links between the programmes were supplied by
a bemused-looking young man, who seemed unconvinced
that the lights weren't about to go out any second, while his
eyes nervously sought to locate which camera he was on. The
programmes were likeable but, to begin with, not brilliant. At

one point prime-time advertising slots were being offered for £50.

To the relief of those who desperately wanted a greater choice of television channel options, Channel 4 survived this early precarious state, and went from strength to strength as the alternative channel, tackling issues and commissioning programmes that could have found no place on the other outlets. Despite inevitable fluctuations in quality, the overall line on the graph was always upwards.

Amid these rocky beginnings, Channel 4 had, however, already laid down a visual statement of intent, with its 'puzzle' logo, designed by Robinson Lambie-Nairn, and its striking animated appearances, the numeral 4 made of nine brightly coloured three-dimensional blocks, which disassembled themselves, revolved then reconfigured, or fell like a technicolour meteorite shower to form the numeral. It is still in use today, most notably in recent years in a series of striking idents where, initially invisible in urban and rural landscapes, it almost magically appears, constructed from elements within that landscape as the camera's point of view shifts.

In 2004, with more than twenty years of broadcasting under its belt, the channel was looking to perpetuate and renew, through design and typography, its credentials as the natural home for the visually innovative. Fontsmith was founded in London in 1999 by Jason Smith. Smith studied lettering, calligraphy and signwriting at college, his passion for type design merging with a similar one for branding. Although Fontsmith continues to develop its library of commercially available fonts, it is in the field of high-profile corporate typographic design that it has become renowned: clients include Sainsbury's, Jaguar, the Premier League, and several television networks. Smith described the Channel 4

abcdefghij
klmnopqrst
uvwxyz

ABCDEFGHI
JKLMNOPQR
STUVWXYZ

CHANNEL 4 HEADLINE IN ITS BOLD WEIGHT.

commission as a game-changer, in that in terms of recognition it was his breakthrough design, award-winning and leading to many more television branding opportunities. His task, as he described it, 'was to design a typeface with a killer quirk to back up the on-air and off-air identities'. The font had to be able to identify the channel without the need for the network logo, to be able to work alongside the in-depth analysis of Channel 4's hour-long evening news as well as with irreverent, boundary challenging comedies; 'bloody hard to get the balance right', as its creator later reflected.

Although adapted versions were created for text and for C4 Learning, it was the headline version that saw the font at its most striking; monoline, angular, yet with the edges softened. It was unpredictable: where straight lines might be expected, it curved, as in the arms of the X, the angle of the L, the leg of the K, the v and w, and the flattened apex of the A. Although in essence a sans serif, serifs occasionally featured, on the I in both cases, the numeral 1, upper-case J, and the oddball tour de force, the r, two serifs at the baseline, but none at the top – no ear or spur there either, just a tight, angular curve. If one character identified the font, it was this one. Quirkiness was further added by the lower-case g, always a chance for the designer to display flair. Smith created a hybrid of the two forms, of the 'spectacles' double loop version, and the tailed one. Even the capital Q managed to have a flourish in its tail despite the tightness and control of the overall design style.

Channel 4 Headline was a sleek, modern, eye-catching but unfussy statement of stylistic intent that complemented and expressed perfectly the sophisticated but unconventional spirit of the network. Launched in January 2005, it remained in place for over ten years, a fine achievement in a medium that constantly re-examines and overhauls its content and scheduling, and which itself, and in the viewing habits and options of its audience, has altered radically in that decade.

Neville Brody (*see* ARCADIA) designed two new fonts, Chadwick, a more standard sans serif for information, and Horseferry for headlines, which debuted in September 2015. As striking as Channel 4 Headline had been, Horseferry, 'designed to reflect on the sharp, disruptive and cutting-edge personality and aesthetic of this unique British institution',

plays off and reacts to its predecessor, with occasional unexpected serifs, and a spikier personality, jagged spurs and ears
on the lower-case r and a, and angular slices being taken out
of the rounded forms of upper-case characters C, D, O and Q.
It was a testing brief to create a design that was as arresting
and unconventional as Jason Smith's, yet had to look distinctively different to it – in terms of perception of the channel's
image and its marketing, a change has to be seen to have taken
place – while still sleekly and elegantly representing Channel
4's personality as the high-quality home of unconventional,
ground-breaking, highly intelligent programming. But typographically, the channel is still in safe hands.

GUARDIAN EGYPTIAN

FIRST APPEARANCE   2005, GREAT BRITAIN

DESIGNERS   CHRISTIAN SCHWARTZ, AMERICAN;
PAUL BARNES, BRITISH

The Guardian newspaper began life as *The Manchester Guardian* in 1821, changing to its current title in 1959. It is financially supported by the Scott Trust, dedicated to ensuring the paper's independence and protecting it from takeover. The paper's political stance has always been to the left of centre, or centre left, and it has been celebrated for its design ever since David Hillman's 1988 redesign, with its ranged-right title-piece combining a serifed italic '*The*' with a bold sans serif 'Guardian'.

Even before the massive speculation in the last few years over the future of the printed newspaper, the industry had been going through some radical self-assessment. Modern life was judged to be less compatible than formerly with the large page size of the broadsheet newspaper. No longer was the paterfamilias spreading his daily read across the dining table, or ensconced in the inviolable territory of his armchair. Such reading might now be done during the daily commute to work, readers squeezed into the restricted elbow room of public transport. Large format had traditionally meant serious news coverage, tabloid format signifying sensational headlines and greater pictorial content. But in the autumn of 2003 both *The Independent* and *The Times* changed to tabloid. *The Guardian* was to follow with a format switch on 12 September 2005, but to a strikingly different size known as Berliner – only slightly wider than tabloid, but with a longer height to the page.

Time for decent Tories to speak up. Our democracy is being rigged

Owen Jones

Mass disenfranchisement, starving the opposition of funds: ministers will do anything to retain power

emocracy is precious: the collective product of centuries of struggle by our ancestors, and forged amid protests, riots and massacres. Those who fought for it were humiliated, ridiculed, attacked and tortured: think of the Levellers and the Chartists, trade unionists and suffragettes, soldiers who drove back the tide of genocidal Nazism - all laid bricks on the foundations of our democracy. Given the sacrifice and effort expended over so many generations, we should be sensitive about serving governments tinkering with our democracy. Alarming, then, that there is all too little scrutiny of a far-reaching attack on a democratic system that was so hard fought f⁻⁻

A new pape⁻ is the sort that unread; but th⁻

Hope Not Hate is warning of "the single biggest act of disenfranchisement in our history". Let's offer a prize - it could be a peerage perhaps - for the first person to guess who benefits from the new system. "As they stand," says the institute, the new registers "favour more affluent rural and semi-rural areas, which have stable populations."

And what of the effect on black and minority ethnic voters? In the 2010 election 68% of them voted Labour compared with just 16% for the Tories, only two points ahead of the Lib Dems. Although registered ethnic minority voters are about as likely to vote as their white counterparts, registration levels can be much lower. While 90% of white people were registered at a current address in 2010, the number dropped to 50% among those of black African

We won't need to wait until 2020 to see the impact: in next year's Scottish, Welsh, London and local elections, says the report, the new system "could have a profound effect". The effect will be on urban voters, private tenants, students and ethnic minorities - in other words, whole chunks of the electorate that are significantly less likely to vote Tory.

Even before boundaries are redrawn on the basis of registers purged disproportionately of non-Tory voters, our electoral system now has a pronounced anti-Labour bias. According to the pollster John Curtice, if Labour and the Tories were exactly tied in number of votes cast, Labour would be 46 seats behind.

Let's not pretend that the Tories don't know exactly what they are doing. As the Tories' house journal, the Daily Telegraph, put it in the immediate aftermath of the general election: "Redrawing constituency boundaries to lock Labour out of power for a decades

> **In the 19th and 20th centuries, laws were enacted to expand the electorate – now it is being shrunk** ""

Guardian Egyptian Text

Guardian Egyptian Headline

PLAIN BUT ELEGANT: VARIOUS WEIGHTS OF GUARDIAN EGYPTIAN AT WORK ON THE PAGE.

The new Berliner format, now with colour throughout, was an opportunity for another complete redesign, and the paper seized it with both hands. Now printed on presses that could cope with pictures running across the gutter of a page spread, giving the possibility of much more dramatic handling of images, the paper would also need an accompanying typographic overhaul.

Previously *The Guardian* had used Helvetica Bold for its headlines, with Miller for the text, a fairly conventional serif and sans serif combination. But for the Berliner, designers Christian Schwartz and Paul Barnes were given the task of producing something bespoke. *Guardian* creative director Mark Porter saw the new format as being 'calmer, more modern'. Paul Barnes worked initially on a sans serif, but became attracted to the idea of producing an Egyptian, a term which has emerged from its confused early nineteenth-century nomenclature to mean a slab serif. What Barnes and Schwartz went on to produce was a face with, in place of true slab serifs that meet the vertical strokes at a right angle, what were in essence truncated wedges, no brackets, meeting the upright strokes at an angle. Typographic contrast, usually sought through the serif and sans serif juxtaposition, was instead achieved using just one face, but in a range of weights from hairline to black, giving multiple options for treating the numerous hierarchies of information on a typical *Guardian* page, with further options provided by the use of colour, whether in the type itself or in the form of coloured panels from which the characters are reversed out. Guardian Egyptian is elegant in all weights from the delicacy of the hairline to the solid insistence of the black. With a generous x-height, there is a sense of rotundity, of openness, especially in the regular weight.

As well as its intrinsic well-crafted forms, Guardian Egyptian's greatness lies in how it quietly and distinctively plays its part in the overall appearance of the paper. As Paul Barnes said of his hoped-for reception of the type during the launch of the Berliner, 'I want people to feel "That's interesting" on the first day and by the third be reading the news again. I want it to be part of their life and for them to feel affection, because that's what people feel towards *The Guardian*.' He and his design partner achieved that objective, but Guardian Egyptian is too fine a design to become completely unnoticeable: in larger text the face always subliminally asserts its personality.

On the cover of *The Guardian*'s final broadsheet edition, anticipating the appearance of the new format following its preview, *The Press Gazette* was quoted: 'It is, as you would expect, a thing of beauty.' *The Evening Standard* commented: 'definitely not a bigger paper shrunk to fit'. This judgement of beauty was and remains accurate. Instantly recognizable by its title-piece, dark blue panel with the name ranged right as before, bold lowercase, '*The*' picked out in pale cyan, 'Guardian' in white, no word space, *The Guardian* is consistent but with daily variety, a low-cost object of beauty every day on the news-stands.

PIEL SCRIPT

FIRST APPEARANCE   2011, ARGENTINA
DESIGNER   ALEJANDRO PAUL, ARGENTINIAN

The early years of the twenty-first century saw the emergence
of South America as a significant and energetic player in the
typographic field. One of the prominent forces has been the
Argentinian foundry Sudtipos, founded in Buenos Aires in
2001. The partnership came about as a by-product of the
worsening economic situation in the country, which reached
crisis point in that year with a freezing of bank accounts and
rioting in protest at the government's ineffectual handling of
the situation. One of those who lost his job was Alejandro
Paul. His background had been in packaging design, and
much of the output of the collective reflects this. 'For example,
when you have to design the front of an ice cream container,
common 'fashion' fonts almost never work exactly the way
you want them right out of the box', he observes in *Creative
Characters: The MyFonts Interviews* (2010). Sudtipos set about
designing fonts specifically for designers, with alternate characters to make designs easier to customize; and alphabets that
would inhabit a given space with ease, comfort and fluidity.

It is perhaps unsurprising that the vast majority of the
collective's range is of script faces, or those which show a
calligraphic element. It is inescapable when looking at them
en masse not to feel that they bring influences into play that
would not be apparent if the designers had been European or
from North America. Paul's cited influences run counter to
this impression: 'Argentine graphic culture is more European

'A STYLISH SKIN SCRIPT' THAT LOOKS SPECTACULAR ON PAPER.

and modernist in character, rather than personalized with scripts.' He cites many of his biggest influences and sources of inspiration as the work of early-twentieth-century lettering artists working in the United States and Canada, and asserts that the predominance of scripts is just 'a personal thing'. There is an exuberance, variety and fluidity to them that makes most of the script designs that have preceded them seem rigid, unmalleable. Their spirit feels Latin, at least to a northern European, and, when one thinks of the scripts used on many shop fascias in parts of Spain, it becomes tempting to narrow this definition down further and say Hispanic.

Piel Script is one of the most frantic, visually vibrant of Paul's designs. But he stresses that designing a good script requires readability, consistency and balance, and Piel has this. Piel means 'skin' in Spanish, and the font came about after Paul had had several requests to design tattoos, and decided to attempt a script for that purpose; 'I had worked in corporate branding for a few years before becoming a type designer, and suddenly I was being asked to become involved in personal branding.' Drawing upon his earlier Burgues Script, and infusing it with influences of American point-of-sale showcard script lettering from the 1930s, the result was what he calls 'a stylish skin script'. Whatever one's opinion of tattoos, any based around Piel would be undeniably striking, combining light and heavy strokes to mesmerizing effect. Scripts or blackletter are favourite tattoo lettering styles, but Paul hated seeing a standard face like Bank Script used, whose cultural baggage seemed entirely inappropri-ate. Piel seems designed to dance on what is an elastic and ever-changing surface, the human body. But such is its beauty, it can work elsewhere too. As Paul says, 'If you decide to use it on your skin, I'll be very flattered. If you decide to use it on your skateboard or book cover, I'll be just as happy.'

LUSHOOTSEED

FIRST APPEARANCE   2009, UNITED STATES

DESIGNER   JULIET SHEN, AMERICAN

Sometimes the disappearance of a language can be the result of
direct action by a dominant group, as well as the consequence
of the non-replacement of its speakers by new generations.
Catalan is an example of the former effect, albeit unsuccessful:
a deliberate attempt at suppression by external forces. A victim
of both negative effects was the Native American language
Lushootseed. Spoken by the Puget Salish tribes in the
greater Puget Sound region around Seattle in north-western
Washington State, the language came under pressure in the
late nineteenth century as missionary and, later, government
boarding schools were established to force the assimilation of
indigenous American peoples into anglophone United States
society. Native American children were removed to boarding
schools and punished for speaking their tribal language. There
was no written tradition in the culture of Lushootseed, which
meant that by the 1960s it was almost lost.

Although recordings of the language had been made in the
1950s, these had been done by Leon Metcalf, a non-linguist.
In the 1960s a University of Washington linguistics student,
Thom Hess, became interested in the Puget Salish culture
and began recording orally transmitted stories and legends
from surviving tribal elders living on the Tulalip reservation,
one of those designated for tribes in the region following
the 1855 Treaty of Port Elliott with the US government. Vi
Hilbert, a member of the Skagit tribe, worked with him to

translate the stories and, with a team of linguists, to produce dictionaries.

Juliet Shen's father was a United Nations translator, so languages were part of her background and upbringing. Born in New York, she gained a Master's degree in type design at the University of Reading in Britain, and taught typography at the School of Visual Concepts in Seattle. When in 2008 the Tulalip Language Department commissioned her to design a font specifically for Lushootseed, the number of fluent native speakers could be counted on both hands. Hess and Hilbert had used as their typeface an adaptation of Times New Roman, with phonetic glyphs attached. The sound of the language has been described as echoes of the tribes' physical environment, of the water and the wind, and the clicking sounds of animals. The reaction of one of the Master's course teachers on seeing Lushootseed's typographic representation was: 'This is a graceful language, but it doesn't look that way.' As Juliet Shen remarked, her brief was 'to get rid of an "adapted" look, and make it appear as if it has always been.'

In designing the font, Shen was drawn towards a non-serif form; firstly because of the serif's roots in European pen-based antecedents, but also because it was found that children learning Lushootseed often transcribed the serifs into their own written letterforms if such a style was used in educational material. She was also conscious that, just as the Master's course teacher had pointed out, aesthetics was an important factor in her design. If use of the language was to be increased, that could be assisted by Lushootseed being visually appealing when written, 'much', she said, 'as a well-designed and beautifully-crafted tool will encourage the apprentice cabinet maker to do fine joining'. The Tulalip Tribes are part of the Salish indigenous peoples of the Pacific North-West coast,

ti?ə? di?ə? ?aci+talbixʷ ?al ti?i+
tuha?kʷ dᶻixʷbid čə+. gʷəl
tus?əs+a+lils ?al tudi? sq́xʷabac.
d(i)+əxʷ tu?ux̌̇. tu+a+lil. gʷəl x̌uxʷi?xʷi?.
gʷəl di+ tudəxʷ?ux̌̇s əlgʷə?. gʷəl
tu+a+lil əlgʷə?.

gʷəl absbədbəda? əlgʷə? absbədbəda?
əlgʷə?. gʷəl ti?i+ ?i+lux̌ bəda?s əlgʷə?
gʷəl ?əsq́ʷuṗq́ʷuṗ. ?əsq́ʷuṗq́ʷuṗ. xʷi?
gʷəjəsəds gʷədəxʷu?ibəšs. gʷəl daẏ
ti?ə? čal̓čaləss. **Lushootseed Sulad**

AN EXCERPT FROM THE SAUK-SUIATTLE TRIBAL STORY 'THE LEGEND OF THE
BOY WHO COULD NOT WALK' SET IN LUSHOOTSEED SULAD. THE EL-BELT
CHARACTER CAN BE SEEN AT THE END OF THE FIRST LINE.

whose homelands stretch from British Columbia into Oregon.
For inspiration Shen looked to Salish art, largely made from
wood, which she saw had 'the symmetry of nature, where lines
curve and there are no true circles'. Shapes were simplified,
with an important relationship between the interior or negative
space, and the perimeter of the object, sensibilities she saw
mirrored in the creation of letterforms. Her designs reflected
this spirit; forms were softer, intersections rounded rather than
pointed.

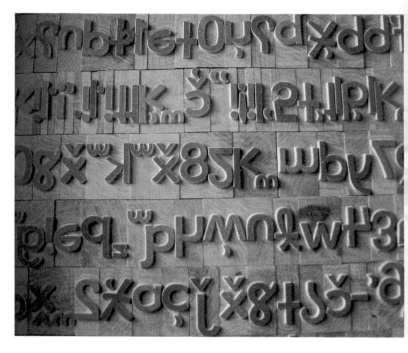

THE WOODEN VERSION OF THE TYPE, CREATED AT THE HAMILTON WOOD
TYPE AND PRINTING MUSEUM.

In designing the characters, she also allowed the preferred
forms of the teachers themselves to override any established
patterns. If the language was to survive, it had to reflect the
preferences of those who are teaching it over any preconceived
approach. The resulting font was called Lushootseed School,
to underline its first, most vital function – to teach. This
approach eased the initial acceptance of the new font by
teachers. Interestingly, however, there is a move now among
users towards the established form of the 'crossed el' character,
called el-belt, where the cross-section is in the shape of a
looped belt. This had originally been overridden by teachers'
preferences as too awkward to write, but was made available

nonetheless in the alternate font version, Lushootseed Sulad. Now, as more colleges offer Lushootseed as a second language, Lushootseed Sulad is replacing Lushootseed School.

After the digital font was completed, Lushootseed School was also produced in wood by Wisconsin's Hamilton Wood Type and Printing Museum. This has enabled the children to have a literally 'hands-on' experience with the language, printing with letterpress and seeing the language as a living, crafted form. It also helps those whose learning and development are better suited to physical and craft skills – which leads us back to Shen's analogy of the apprentice cabinetmaker and their tools. She sees aesthetics as a crucial factor in what she concedes is an 'uphill' struggle to preserve this and similar languages. However, there is progress: 2010 saw the start of an annual series of Lushootseed language conferences at Seattle University, and courses in Lushootseed language and literature are offered at Northwest Indian College in Bellingham and Evergreen State College in Olympia, and are planned at the University of Washington in Seattle.

ZULIA

FIRST APPEARANCE 2013
DESIGNER JOSE LUIS JOLUVIAN, VENEZUELAN

The twenty-first century has seen a rebirth in the popularity of
the script face, both in the number of new ones that have been
designed, and in their consequent usage. Of the three basic
typographic groupings of scripts, serifs and sans serifs, it is
scripts that see the least usage, and that are usually only lightly
represented in type companies' lists.

For the designer, the problem with scripts has been that
although they were supposed to offer a freer, natural, handwritten style of lettering, most turned out in practice to be more
rigid and constricting than sans serifs and serifs. There was little
room for any play with letterspacing, because the characters
needed to connect. There often seemed to be something oddly
intractable to them as shapes once formed into words, shapes
not enhanced by the customary large contrast in height between
the x-height and the cap height. Rarely did it feel as though
they were dancing across the page – more often the effect was of
a leaden slouch. To make things worse, upper-case letters could
be equivocal, to put it mildly, in terms of legibility.

The German designer and typographer Jan Tschichold,
in his 1946 *An Illustrated History of Writing and Lettering*,
provided a possible explanation for this, blaming eighteenth-
century 'seductive engraved copy-books', where a florid
overdecorative style had emerged owing little to genuine
penmanship. The copperplate style, and commercial script,
was a further distortion of this, using 'regular alternation

> *Daría valor a las cosas, no por lo que valen, sino por lo que significan.*

ZULIA: RHYTHM AND A SENSE OF SOLIDITY, EXUDING A CONFIDENCE IN ITS OWN EXTRAVAGANCE.

of fine and thick strokes [to disguise] the unnatural writing technique'.

Aesthetic baggage could be a problem too. R.S. Hutchings, in *A Manual of Script Typefaces* (1965), commented: 'Until well into the 1930s it was exceptional for even a well-stocked composing room to hold more than a single script series, and their use was restricted almost exclusively to the circumscribed field of professional and social stationery', by which he meant wedding invitations, and the lifeless, off-the-peg sophistication to which designer Michael Bierut alludes with unconcealed distaste in Gary Hustwit's *Helvetica* film, describing the pre-Helvetica world of corporate letter-heads: 'maybe a script typeface ... the nuptial script and the ivory paper'.

Later, more informal styles emerged, based on letters written with a brush, or upon contemporary handwriting. Several have become standards on computer operating systems: for example, Brush Script, a 1940s' American Type Founders advertising face by Robert E. Smith, and the celebrated Mistral of Roger Excoffon (1953), a handwriting-style script that belonged, says Julien Gineste in *Roger Excoffon et la Fonderie Olive*, 'to the "civilization" of the ballpoint pen' (*see* CALYPSO *and* ANTIQUE OLIVE).

The recent growth in popularity is due to at least two factors. During the 1990s the complete dominance of computer-generated design made other methods look obsolete. But designers tired of the look of design that anyone with the software and the skills to use it can do, and with it their clients and target audiences. The early 2000s saw a move, spiritually, back to the personal and the handcrafted. The latter also chimed with a post-global economic meltdown, do-it-yourself aesthetic that has also seen a rise in popularity of traditional homemaking crafts previously considered mori-bund, such as sewing and knitting.

Developments in type-designing software, the OpenType technology that gives type designers the ability to create multiple characters, has allowed scripts to shake off the rigidity of the past, giving a font's user the ability to add a variety to words that far better represents the idea of something written by hand. Also, as Tschichold would have surely concurred, basing the design of the font on natural, handmade strokes can be an advantage too.

You can probably see more connecting and brush scripts in one place at the website of the Argentinian collective Sudtipos than anywhere else, or at any point in history (*see* PIEL SCRIPT). Among them is Zulia, created by Madrid-based Venezuelan graphic designer and lettering artist Jose Luis Joluvian. Named after his home state, Venezuela's most western, Zulia was created by handmade strokes on paper using brush and marker. These were then used in a modular way to create characters; in the lower case the repetition of certain strokes can be easily seen. These give Zulia its rhythm and a sense of solidity, reassurance, a confidence in its own extravagance, what Sudtipos calls 'a heavier type, contrasted and low-rise'. Yet the way the upper areas of the lower case bounce above and below a notional x-height gives a constant sense of energy.

It's not an immediate comparison to make perhaps, but Zulia shares a crucial quality with Helvetica, particularly the bolder weights of the Swiss giant, in that it gives a feeling of occupying its space beautifully. It's a quality often absent in scripts, but Zulia has it in abundance. It is also extremely legible, in both upper and lower case. The characters sit like rich, ripe fruit from some near-equatorial forest. Too rich for chilly, north European shores? It doesn't matter. A feast for the eyes, Zulia manages to be both practical and celebratory, a rare combination. It takes the form of the script, and makes it richer, more visually satisfying. It simply looks and feels right.

BIBLIOGRAPHY

Avis, F.C., *Edward Philip Prince: Type Punchcutter*, F.C. Avis, London, 1967.

Balius, Andreu, 'Super Veloz: A Creative Response to a Typographic Crisis', *Ultrabold* 2, Spring 2007.

Ball, Johnson, *William Caslon: Master of Letters*, Roundwood Press, Kineton, 1973.

Barker, Nicolas, *Stanley Morison*, Macmillan, London, 1972.

Beaujon, Paul, 'The "Garamond" Types: Sixteenth and Seventeenth Century Sources Considered', *The Fleuron* 5, 1926.

Berliner, Harold, Nicolas Barker, Jim Rimmer and John Dreyfus, 'Starling Burgess, No Type Designer: A Rebuttal of Some Allegations and Suppositions Made by Mike Parker in His Article "Starling Burgess, Type Designer" in *Printing History* 31/32 (1994)', *Printing History* 37, vol. XIX, no. 1, 1998.

Blumenthal, Joseph, *Bruce Rogers: A Life in Letters 1870–1957*, W.Thomas Taylor, Austin TX, 1989.

Branigan, Tania, 'An Egyptian Dynasty, Founded on Letters, Is Meticulously but Quietly Restored', *The Guardian*, 10 September 2005, www.theguardian.com.

Briggs, R.C.H., *Sir Emery Walker: A Memoir*, University of Tampa Press, Tampa FL, 2011.

Bruckner, D.J.R., *Frederic Goudy*, Harry N. Abrams, New York, 1990.

Bryans, Dennis, '"A tolerable interpreter": Robert Bell and the Chinese on the Ballarat Goldfields', *La Trobe Journal* 92, 2013.

Burin, Margaret, 'Chinese Goldfields History Returned Home', www.abc.net.au.

Burke, Christopher, *Paul Renner: The Art of Typography*, Hyphen Press, London, 1998.

Carter, Harry, *A View of Early Typography up to about 1600: The Lyell Lectures 1968*, Oxford University Press, Oxford, 1969.

Chamaret, Sandra, Julien Gineste and Sébastien Morlighem, *Roger Excoffon et la Fonderie Olive*, Ypsilon Editeur, Paris, 2010.

Channel 4 Headline: story of the font's development at www.fontsmith.com.

Cinamon, Gerald, *Rudolf Koch: Letterer, Type Designer, Teacher*, Oak Knoll Press, New Castle DE, 2000.

Clair, Colin, *A History of European Printing*, Academic Press, London, 1976.

Cobden-Sanderson, T.J., *The Journals of Thomas James Cobden-Sanderson, 1879–1922*, Burt Franklin, New York, 1969.

Connare, Vincent, 'I Hate Comic Sans', *Ultrabold* 5, Autumn 2008.

Consuegra, David, *American Type: Design and Designers*, Allworth Press, New York, 2004.

Cost, Patricia A., *The Bentons: How an American Father and Son Changed the Printing Industry*, Cary Graphics Arts Press, Rochester NY, 2011.

Farey, Dave, 'Travelling Light: A New Face for American Signage', *Ultrabold* 12, Autumn 2012.

Farey, Dave, 'A Life and Times', *Ultrabold* 15, Spring 2014.

Friedman, Russell, *Out of Darkness: The Story of Louis Braille*, Clarion Books, New York, 1997.

Gill, Eric, *Autobiography*, Plantin, Cardiff, 1995 (1940).

Goudy, Frederic, *Goudy's Type Designs: His Story and Specimens*, Myriade Press, New Rochelle

NY, 1978; originally published as *A Half-Century of Type Design and Typography, 1895–1945*, The Typophiles, New York, 1946.

Green, Robert, 'Reviving the Doves Type', *Ultrabold* 12, Autumn 2012.

Haley, Allen, *ABC's of Type*, Watson Guptil, New York, 1990.

Harling, Robert, *The Letter Forms and Type Designs of Eric Gill*, Eva Svensson, Westerham, 1976.

Hirasuna, Delphine, 'Designing a Font to Preserve a Vanishing Language, *@issue: The Online Journal of Business and Design*, 13 October 2009, www.atissuejournal.com.

Howes, Justin, *Johnston's Underground Type*, Capital Transport, London, 2000.

Hustwit, Gary, *Helvetica: A Documentary Film by Gary Hustwit*, Plexifilm, 2007.

Hutchings, R.S., *A Manual of Script Typefaces: A Definitive Guide to Series in Current Use*, Cory, Adams & McKay, London, 1965.

Ing, Janet, *Johann Gutenberg and His Bible*, The Typophiles, New York, 1988.

Jay, Leonard (ed.), *Letters of the Famous 18th Century Printer John Baskerville of Birmingham: Together With a Bibliography of Works Printed by Him at Birmingham*, Birmingham School of Printing, 1932.

Johnston, Edward, *Writing and Illuminating, and Lettering*, Pitman, London, 1977 (1906).

Johnston, Priscilla, *Edward Johnston*, Barrie & Jenkins, London, 1959.

Kelly, Jerry, *The First Flowering: Bruce Rogers at the Riverside Press 1896–1912*, David R. Godine, Boston MA, 2009.

Kelly, Jerry, and Misha Beletsky, 'The Noblest Roman: A History of the Centaur Types of Bruce Rogers', unpublished, 2015.

Kelly, Rob Roy, *American Wood Type, 1828–1900: Notes on the Evolution of Decorated and Large Types and Comments on Related Trades of the Period*, Van Nostrand Reinhold, New York, 1969.

Kelly, Rob Roy, American Wood Type collection, University of Texas at Austin, www.utexas.edu.

Lester, Valerie, *Giambattista Bodoni: His Life and His World*, David R. Godine, Boston MA, 2015.

Loxley, Simon, 'Motorway Madness: David Kindersley and the Great Road Sign Ruckus', *Type: The Secret History of Letters*, I.B.Tauris, London, 2004.

Loxley, Simon, 'The World's Favourite Font!?', *Design Week*, vol. 23, no. 41, 9 October 2008.

Loxley, Simon, 'From the Library Archives (The Occupied Times)', *Ultrabold* 11, Spring 2012.

Loxley, Simon, *Printer's Devil: The Life and Work of Frederic Warde*, David R. Godine, Boston MA, 2013.

Loxley, Simon (ed.), *Believe Me, I Am: Selected Letters of Frederic Warde, 1921–1939*, Simon Loxley, Woodbridge, Suffolk, 2015.

MacCarthy, Fiona, *Eric Gill*, Faber & Faber, London, 1989.

MacCarthy, Fiona, *William Morris: A Life for Our Time*, Faber & Faber, London, 1994.

Maggs, Simon, 'The True Story about Westminster (the Font!)', www.mercerdesign.com.

Magno, Alessandro Marzo, *Bound in Venice: The Serene Republic and the Dawn of the Book*, Europa Editions, New York, 2013.

Mason, John, *J.H. Mason RDI: A Selection from the Notebooks of a Scholar-printer Made by His Son John Mason*, Twelve by Eight Press, Leicester, 1961.

Meynell, Francis, *English Printed Books*, Collins, London, 1946.

Middendorp, Jan (ed.), *Creative Characters: The MyFonts Interviews*, vol. 1, Bis Publishers, Amsterdam, 2010.

Monotype, 'New Series of the Centaur Types of Bruce Rogers and the Arrighi Italics of Frederic Warde', Monotype specimen,

Lanston Monotype Corporation, London, 1929.

Morison, Stanley, *Four Centuries of Fine Printing: Two Hundred and Seventy-two Examples of the Work of Presses Established between 1465 and 1924*, Ernest Benn, London, 1949 (1924).

Mortimer, Ian, and James Mosley, *Ornamented Types: Twenty-three Alphabets from the Foundry of Louis John Pouchée*, I.M. Imprimit/ St Bride Printing Library, London, 1992–93.

Mosley, James, 'The Early Career of William Caslon', *Journal of the Printing Historical Society*, London, 1967.

Mosley, James, *The Nymph and the Grot: The Revival of the Sanserif Letter*, Friends of the St Bride Printing Library, London, 1999.

Mosley, James, 'Garamond or Garamont?', typefoundry.blogspot. co.uk, 2011, 2012.

Mouron, Henri, *Cassandre*, Thames & Hudson, London, 1985.

Pankow, David, 'A Face by Any Other Name Is Still My Face: A Tale of Type Piracy', *Printing History*, vol. XIX, no. 1, 1998.

Pardoe, F.E., *John Baskerville of Birmingham: Letter-founder and Printer*, Frederic Muller, London, 1975.

Parker, Mike, 'W. Starling Burgess, Type Designer?', *Printing History* 31/32, vol. XVI, nos 1 and 2, 1994.

Paul, Alejandro, Piel Script font description and history, www. sudtipos.com.

Poyner, Rick, 'Reputations: Jonathan Barnbrook, Virus', interview, *Eye* magazine, Winter 1994, www. eyemagazine.com.

Rodenberg, Julius, 'Karl Klingspor', *The Fleuron*, 1926.

Rutherfurd, J., *William Moon, LL.D., and His Work for the Blind*, Hodder & Stoughton, London, 1898.

Schalansky, Judith, *Fraktur Mon Amour*, Verlag Hermann Schmidt Mainz, Mainz, 2006.

Scholderer, Victor, *Johann Gutenberg: The Inventor of Printing*, The Trustees of the British Museum, London, 1963.

Shen, Juliet, 'Aesthetic Innovation in Indigenous Typefaces: Designing a Lushootseed Font, *Glimpse* 7, Autumn 2010 www.glimpsejournal. com.

Shields, David 'A Short History of the Italian', *Ultrabold* 4, Spring 2008.

Steinberg, S.H., *Five Hundred Years of Printing*, The British Library, London, 1955, rev. 1996.

The Book of Oz Cooper: An Appreciation of Oswald Bruce Cooper, Society of Typographic Arts, Chicago, 1949.

Thrift, Julia, 'Roger Excoffon,' *Baseline* 14, Esselte Letraset, London, 1991.

Thurman, Judith, 'A Loss for Words: What Happens When a Language Dies?', *New Yorker*, 30 March 2015.

Tschichold, Jan, *An Illustrated History of Writing and Lettering*, Zwemmer, London, 1946.

Wang, Yewang, and Julia Ryder, 'An "Eccentric" Paper Edited for the Unwelcome Aliens: A Study of the Earliest Australian Chinese Newspaper, *The Chinese Advertiser*', Australian Academic and Research Libraries, Australian Library and Information Association, Canberra, December 1999.

Warde, Beatrice *The Crystal Goblet: Sixteen Essays on Typography*, The Sylvan Press, London, 1955.

Warde, Beatrice, 'Early Years and the Influence of Henry Lewis Bullen', *The Monotype Recorder*, vol. 44, no. 1, Autumn 1970.

Wershler-Henry, Darren, *The Iron Whim: A Fragmented History of Typewriting*, Cornell University Press, Ithaca NY, 2005.

Windisch, Albert, 'The Work of Rudolf Koch', *The Fleuron*, 1928.

Zaczek, Iain, *Essential William Morris*, Dempsey Parr, London, 1999.

Zulia, font description and history, www.sudtipos.com.

PICTURE CREDITS

GUTENBERG'S BIBLE TYPE   Oxford, Bodleian Library, Arch. B b.11, fol. 162r

JENSON'S ROMAN TYPE   Oxford, Bodleian Library, Arch. G b.6 fol. 6r

ALDINE ITALICS   Oxford, Bodleian Library, Auct. 2 R 7.3

FRACTUR   Oxford, Bodleian Library, John Johnson Collection of Printed Ephemera, John Fraser Collection

GARAMOND   courtesy of St Bride Library

CASLON & CASLON'S ENGLISH ARABICK   Oxford, Bodleian Library, Gough Maps 41f (60)

BASKERVILLE   Oxford, Bodleian Library, Don. D.185

BODONI   Oxford, Bodleian Library, Arch. BB c.2,3 Robert Thorne / W Thorowg

FAT FACE ITALIC   courtesy of St Bride Library

TWO LINES ENGLISH EGYPTIAN   courtesy of St Bride Library

POUCHÉE'S 18 LINES NO. 2   courtesy of St Bride Library

BRAILLE   courtesy of St Bride Library; photo Simon Loxley

CHINESE ADVERTISER CHARACTERS   COURTESY of Dennis Bryans

FRENCH ANTIQUE   courtesy of St Bride Library, Simon Loxley

TYPEWRITER   © Penguin Publishing Group (draft)

GOLDEN TYPE   Oxford, Bodleian Library, Kelmscott Press e.1 / page 101r

DOVES TYPE   Oxford, Bodleian Library, Broxb. 51.10

ARNOLD BÖCKLIN   Dave Farey

CLOISTER BLACK   courtesy of St Bride Library

CENTAUR   Simon Loxley

GOUDY OLD STYLE   courtesy of St Bride Library

LONDON UNDERGROUND   courtesy of St Bride Library; photo Simon Loxley

SOUVENIR   courtesy of St Bride Library

COOPER BLACK   courtesy of easyJet

NEULAND   Simon Loxley

ARRIGHI   Simon Loxley

FUTURA   courtesy of St Bride Library

BROADWAY   Dave Farey

GILL SANS   courtesy of St Bride Library

TIMES NEW ROMAN   courtesy of St Bride Library

PEIGNOT   Oxford, Bodleian Library, Limited Editions Club 104/1

STENCIL   Simon Loxley

SUPER VELOZ   Andreu Balius

HELVETICA   courtesy of St Bride Library; photo Simon Loxley

CALYPSO   courtesy of St Bride Library; photo Simon Loxley

TRANSPORT   courtesy of St Bride Library

ANTIQUE OLIVE   courtesy of St Bride Library

DATA 70   Dave Farey

BLOODY HELL   Dave Farey

ARCADIA   Simon Loxley

MASON   Simon Loxley

NATWEST   courtesy of Freda Sack

COMIC SANS   courtesy of Bunch Design

AMANAR   Pierre di Sciullo

CHANNEL 4 FONTS   Fontsmith

GUARDIAN EGYPTIAN   Copyright Guardian News & Media Ltd 2016; font samples courtesy of Christian Schwartz and Commercial Type

PIEL SCRIPT   courtesy of Alejandro Paul

LUSHOOTSEED   Specimen courtesy of Juliet Shen; photo Hamilton Wood Type and Printing Museum, Wisconsin

ZULIA   Simon Loxley

INDEX